DATE DUE

Iris Murdoch

IRIS MURDOCH

Modern Critical Views

These and other titles in preparation

Modern Critical Views

IRIS MURDOCH

Edited and with an introduction by
Harold Bloom
Sterling Professor of the Humanities
Yale University

CHELSEA HOUSE PUBLISHERS ◦ 1986
New York ◦ New Haven ◦ Philadelphia

© 1986 by Chelsea House Publishers, a division of Chelsea
House Educational Communications, Inc.

133 Christopher Street, New York, NY 10014
345 Whitney Avenue, New Haven, CT 06511
5014 West Chester Pike, Edgemont, PA 19028

Introduction © 1986 by Harold Bloom

Printed and bound in the United States of America

∞   The paper used in this publication meets the minimum
requirements of the American National Standard for
Permanence of paper for Printed Library Materials, Z39.48-1984.

Library of Congress Cataloging-in-Publication Data
Main entry under title:

Iris Murdoch.

(Modern critical views)
Bibliography: p.
Includes index.
1. Murdoch, Iris—Criticism and interpretation—Addresses, essays,
lectures. I. Bloom, Harold. II. Title.
III. Series.
PR6063.U7Z7   1986   823'.914   86-947
ISBN 0-87754-705-X (alk. paper)

Contents

Editor's Note

This book gathers together a representative selection of the best criticism available upon the novels of Iris Murdoch, arranged in the chronological order of its original publication. I am grateful to Peter Childers and Ingrid Holmberg for their assistance in editing this volume.

The introduction analyzes Murdoch's most recent novel, *The Good Apprentice*, while surveying also the moral stance of her work, particularly in the religious dimension. It is followed here by Murdoch's own polemical essay "Against Dryness," which serves as the manifesto for her career as a novelist.

Frederick J. Hoffman begins the chronological sequence with a brief reading of *The Italian Girl* in the context of Murdoch's earlier novels. This prelude on her first phase is followed here by Frank Kermode's meditation upon *Bruno's Dream*, which seems to me Murdoch's first permanent achievement as a fiction. In an exegesis of *The Nice and the Good*, Frank Baldanza explores the evolution of Murdoch's development as a religious novelist, up to that point.

The synoptic overview of Murdoch's London novels by the distinguished scholar of the meditative tradition in English literature, Louis L. Martz, celebrates her as the legitimate heir and continuator of Charles Dickens, seer of London. This high estimate is substantiated by Martz particularly in his remarks on *A Fairly Honourable Defeat*.

Murdoch's Dublin background, with its place in Anglo-Irish tradition, is handled only in *The Red and the Green*, studied here by Donna Gerstenberger in its historical context of the Easter Rising of 1916. With Zohreh Tawakuli Sullivan's analysis of the topos of the demonic in Murdoch's fiction, we are returned to her second novel, *The Flight from the Enchanter*, which establishes the figure of the charismatic "alien God" in much of Murdoch's subsequent work.

The novelist A. S. Byatt, who seems to me the most advanced of

Murdoch's critics, studies the complexities of Shakespearean plot in the early and middle work. In Steven G. Kellman's investigation of *Under the Net*, Murdoch's first novel, we are returned to the origins of her art, the Sartrean existentialism that has been subsumed by her mature and highly individual Platonism. *A Severed Head*, as a crucial transitional novel in that development, is explored here by Ann Gossman in its relation to a parable in Murdoch's ethical treatise, *The Sovereignty of Good*.

Lorna Sage's implicit realization of Murdoch's Platonism informs her perceptions of *Henry and Cato*. The literary convention of the Gothic, one of Murdoch's obsessive resources, is investigated by Dorothy A. Winsor as the medium by which Murdoch represents the psychic perils of a purely narcissistic sexuality. Elizabeth Dipple, Murdoch's most comprehensive scholar, contributes a revealing exegesis of the myth of Apollo and Marsyas in *The Black Prince*, which seems to me to stand with *The Good Apprentice* as the novelist's finest achievement in her ongoing career. Finally, *A Word Child,* one of Murdoch's best books, is analyzed by Richard Todd as a significant realization on the novelist's part that tragedy is an experiential rather than a literary mode.

Introduction

At the end of her first book, an enduring study of Sartre published in 1953, Iris Murdoch prophetically lamented that Sartre's "inability to write a great novel is a tragic symptom of a situation which afflicts us all." Her own inability has extended now through twenty-two novels, of which the best seem to me *Bruno's Dream* (1969), *The Black Prince* (1973), *A Word Child* (1975), and her latest, *The Good Apprentice*. So fecund and exuberant is Murdoch's talent that many more novels may be expected from her. If *The Good Apprentice* marks the start of her strongest phase, and it may, then a great novel could yet come, rather surprisingly in the incongruous form of the nineteenth-century realistic novel. The age of Samuel Beckett and Thomas Pynchon, post-Joycean and post-Faulknerian, is set aside by Murdoch's novelistic procedures, almost as though she thus chose to assert her own direct continuity with the major nineteenth-century Russian and British masters of fiction.

Murdoch's anachronistic style and outmoded narrative devices are not, in my experience of reading her, the principal flaws in her work. Like Gabriel García Márquez, she favors a realism that can be more phantasmagoric than naturalistic, but she tends not to be able to sustain this mixed mode, whereas he can. Consistency of stance is one of Murdoch's problems. She is both fantasist and realist, each on principle, but her abrupt modulations between the two visions sometimes seem less than fully controlled. Her novels rush by us, each a successful entertainment, but none perhaps fully distinct from the others in our memories.

Yet her fictions fuse into a social cosmos, one that is reasonably recognizable as contemporary British upper-middle-class. Of all her talents, the gift of plotting is the most formidable, including a near-Shakespearean faculty for intricate double plots. Again her strength seems sometimes uncontrolled, and even the most responsive reader can feel harried and at last indifferent as labyrinthine developments work themselves through. Yet that

1

is how Murdoch tends to manifest her considerable exuberance as a writer, rather than in the creation of endless otherness in her characters, which nevertheless (and rather sadly) seems to constitute her largest ambition. She does not excel at fresh invention of personalities. We learn to expect certain basic types to repeat themselves in her novels: fierce, very young women, compulsive and cunning, violent in their pursuit of much older men, are omnipresent. Their quarry, those older men, are narcissistic charmers but weak, self-indulgent, hesitant skeptics, fearful of reality. Then there are the power figures whom Murdoch once called "alien gods." These are frequently male, Middle European, Jewish charismatics, who may be presumed to have some allegorical or ironic link to the writer Elias Canetti, a friend of Murdoch in her youth. Unfulfilled older women abound also; they are marked by resentment, identity anxieties, and by a tendency to fall in love drastically, absurdly, and abruptly.

Murdoch's particular mastery is in representing the maelstrom of falling in love, which is the characteristic activity of nearly all her men and women, who somehow have time for busy professional careers in London while obsessively suffering convulsive love relationships. Somewhere in one of her early novels, Murdoch cannily observes that falling out of love is one of the great human experiences, a kind of rebirth in which we see the world with freshly awakened eyes. Though an academic philosopher earlier in her career, Murdoch's actual philosophical achievement is located where she clearly wishes it to be, in her novels, which demonstrate her to be a major student of Eros, not of the stature of Freud or Proust, but still an original and endlessly provocative theorist of the tragicomedy of sexual love, with its peculiar hell of jealousy and self-hatred. Her nearest American equivalent in this dark area is Saul Bellow, a novelist whom otherwise she does not much resemble.

Indeed, she resembles no other contemporary novelist, in part because she is essentially a religious fabulist, of an original and unorthodox sort, and therefore very unlike Graham Greene or John Updike or Walker Percy or Cynthia Ozick, whose varied religious outlooks are located in more definite normative traditions. Murdoch thinks for herself theologically as well as philosophically, and her conceptual originality is difficult for readers to apprehend, particularly when it is veiled by her conventional forms of story-telling and her rather mixed success in the representation of original characters. There is a perpetual incongruity between Murdoch's formulaic procedures and her spiritual insights, an incongruity that continues in *The Good Apprentice*.

The good apprentice is twenty-year-old Edward Baltram, a university student who begins the novel by slyly feeding a drug-laden sandwich to his best friend and fellow-student Mark Wilsden. While Edward goes off to make love to a girl in the neighborhood, Mark wakes up and falls or jumps out of the window to his death. Edward's grief and guilt dominate the book, which is his quest for a secular absolution at the hands of his actual father, Jesse Baltram, an insane vitalist and reclusive painter who begat Edward upon one of his models and subsequently has not seen his son apart from a childhood meeting or two. Murdoch's ironic opening sentence is the novel's spiritual signature:

> I will arise and go to my father, and will say unto him, Father
> I have sinned against heaven and before thee, and am no more
> worthy to be called thy son.

In a narrative that chronicles Edward's journey from hell to purgatory, we might expect that Edward would encounter at least one figure who unequivocally embodies love, wisdom, or at least power. But that underestimates Murdoch's authentic spiritual originality which has now matured to the point that all such figures are negated. Though Edward regards himself as a dead soul, he is nevertheless the book's only legitimate representative of the good, in however apprentice a guise. His elders all fail him, and themselves are exposed as souls deader than he is. Jesse Baltram, his mad father, is a magician but a perpetually dying one until his mysterious death by water. Mother May, Jesse's wife, seems at first as charming and innocent as her daughters, Bettina and Ilona, Edward's half-sisters, and the long middle section of the book set at Seegard, Jesse's estate, begins as the most beautiful of all Murdoch's pastoral idylls. But May is revealed to be scheming, resentful, and jealous, Bettina scarcely less so, and the ineffable Ilona is transmogrified into a Soho stripper. The book's wisdom figure, Thomas McCaskerville, Edward's uncle by marriage, is at once a subtle Scottish-Jewish psychoanalyst, uttering a parodistic version of R. D. Laing's madness-as-spiritual-journey ideology, and also a bemused cuckold, preaching about the reality principle of death while understanding very little of life as it touches him most closely.

With her alien gods and charismatics so discredited, Murdoch boldly steps into their place herself, editorializing directly about her characters' psychological and spiritual miseries. Here she analyzes the meditative stance of Stuart, Edward's step-brother and foil, who also has rejected life in favor of a death that might precede a more abundant life:

> A disinterested observer might have wondered why Stuart so
> ardently rejected God, since he did not simply sit and meditate,

he also knelt down, sometimes even prostrated himself. Once again, Stuart, recognising no problem, instinctively resolved apparent contradictions. Meditation was refuge, quietness, purification, replenishing, return to whiteness. Prayer was struggle, reflection, self-examination, it was more particular, involving concern about other people and naming of names. Harry had said that Stuart wanted to be like Job, always guilty before God, an exalted form of sadomasochism. Stuart's rejection of God was, in effect, his rejection of that "old story," to use Ursula's words, as alien to his being. His mind refused it, spewed it out, not as a dangerous temptation, but as alien tissue. Of course he wanted to be "good"; and so he wanted to avoid guilt and remorse, but those states did not *interest* him. Towards his sins and failures he felt cold, no warmth was generated there. So little did he feel himself menaced from that quarter that in prayer he would even say (for he used words) *dominus et deus*, without attaching the old meaning to those dread sounds. (Perhaps it was important that the words were Latin, not English.) He knew there was no supernatural being and did not design to try to attach the concept in any way to his absolutes. If something, "good" or something, was his "master," it was in no personal or reciprocal relation. His language was thus indeed odd as when he sometimes said "forgive me," or "help me," or when he commended others, Edward for instance, to the possibility of being helped. Stuart understood the phrase "love is only of God"; his love went out into the cosmos as a lonely signal, but also miraculously could return to earth. His belief that his supplication for Edward, his concern for Edward, could help Edward was not a hypothesis about actions which he might, as a result of well-intentioned thoughts, later perform for his brother (though this aspect of the matter was not excluded); nor of course was he resorting to some paranormal telepathic form of healing. He simply felt sure that the purer his love the more efficacious it would be in some "immediate" sense which put in question the ordinary pit-pat of time.

Admirers of Murdoch are fond of defending such authorial interpolations by citing their prevalence in the nineteenth-century novel. It is certainly true that George Eliot is never more impressive than in such interventions, and Murdoch indeed is recognizably in Eliot's explicitly moral tradition.

Unfortunately, what worked sublimely for Eliot cannot work so well for Murdoch, despite her engaging refusal to be self-conscious about her belatedness. As speculation, this paragraph is impressive, but as fiction it makes us wonder why Murdoch *tells us* what we expect her to *show us*. Her gifts for dramatic action are considerable, but her own narrative voice lacks George Eliot's authority, being too qualified and fussy when a rugged simplicity is required. She is no less acute a moral analyst than Eliot, but she does not persuade us that her judgments are a necessary part of the story she has made for us.

Yet I do not wish to slight her conceptual strength as a religious writer, which is her particular excellence, since she has taught herself how subtly story and magic, narrative art and the questing spirit, can fuse in a novel, even if the fusion is incomplete so far in her work. Starting as an existentialist writer in *Under the Net*, she has evolved into that curious oxymoron, a Platonist novelist, perpetually in pursuit of the Good, a quest that she herself parodies in the hilarious and painful couplings of her erotomaniac protagonists. Her obsessive symbol for this sadomasochistic pattern is the myth of Apollo and Marsyas, which was exploited in *The Black Prince* and several other novels, and which is repeated in *The Good Apprentice*. Marsyas the musician, having challenged Apollo to a music contest, loses and suffers the penalty of being flayed to death. Murdoch reads the myth so that the agony of Marsyas is our agony now in seeking to know God in an age when God is dead. So, in *The Good Apprentice*:

> Thomas recalled Edward's weird exalted stare, his uncanny smile. A demon who had nothing to do with the well-being of the ordinary "real" Edward had for a moment looked out. How ambiguous such conditions were. The entranced face of the tortured Marsyas, as Apollo kneels lovingly to tear his skin off, prefigures the death and resurrection of the soul.

Our shudder here is not shared by Murdoch, whose version of a post-Christian religion is marked by violence and deathliness. Whatever Socrates meant by saying we should study dying, Murdoch harshly means that death is the truth, since it destroys every image and every story. Her savage Platonism in the novels is consistent with her stance in *The Fire and the Sun: Why Plato Banished the Artists* (1977):

> Escape from the Cave and approach to the Good is a progressive discarding of relative false goods, of hypotheses, images, and shadows, eventually seen as such.

These are the accents not just of a Platonic exegesis, but of Murdoch's firmest beliefs, expressed overtly in the closing paragraph of *The Fire and the Sun*:

> Plato feared the consolations of art. He did not offer a consoling theology. His psychological realism depicted God as subjecting mankind to a judgment as relentless as that of the old Zeus, although more just. A finely meshed moral causality determines the fate of the soul. That the movement of the saving of Eros is toward an impersonal pictureless void is one of the paradoxes of a complete religion. To present the idea of God at all, even as myth, is a consolation, since it is impossible to defend this image against the prettifying attentions of art. Art will mediate and adorn, and develop magical structures to conceal the absence of God or his distance. We live now amid the collapse of many such structures, and as religion and metaphysics in the West withdraw from the embraces of art, we are it might seem being forced to become mystics through the lack of any imagery which could satisfy the mind. Sophistry and magic break down at intervals, but they never go away and there is no end to their collusion with art and to the consolations which, perhaps fortunately for the human race, they can provide; and art, like writing and like Eros, goes on existing for better and for worse.

This bitter Platonism resembles that of Simone Weil, a powerful early influence upon Murdoch. Whatever one thinks of the spiritual stance of Weil and Murdoch (I personally find it repellant), it seems at once antithetical to the interests of art yet also a powerful goad to Murdoch's development as a novelist who exploits magic while endlessly disowning it.

The Good Apprentice seems to me an advance upon all of Murdoch's previous novels, even *The Black Prince*, because the morally ferocious Platonist finally has allowed herself a wholly sympathetic protagonist in the self-purging Edward. His progress out of an inner hell has no false consolations or illusory images haunting it. In some sense, Edward's achievement and torment is wholly Freudian in its spirit, resembling as it does the later Freud of *Beyond the Pleasure Principle* through *Civilization and Its Discontents*. Freud's last vestige of Platonism, his only transcendentalism, was his worship of reality testing or the reality principle, which was his way of naming the conditions imposed by the outwardness of the world, whose final form is death. Murdoch's only consistent transcendentalism is grimly parallel to Freud's, since her novels insist that religious consciousness, in our post-religious era, must begin with the conviction that only death centers life, that death is the only valid representation of a life better than the life-in-death we all suffer daily.

This is the impressive if rather stark structure that Murdoch imposes upon *The Good Apprentice*, where the first section is called "The Prodigal Son," and depicts Edward's descent into a private hell, and the second, "Seegard," recounts his purgatorial search for his enigmatic magician of a father. The third and last part Murdoch names "Life After Death," implying that the still anguished Edward has begun an ascent into the upper reaches of his personal purgatory.

Like nearly all of her twenty-two novels, Murdoch's *The Good Apprentice* has a surface that constitutes a brilliant entertainment, a social comedy of and for the highly literate. Beneath that surface an astringent post-Christian Platonism has evolved into a negative theology that pragmatically offers only the Gnostic alternatives of either total libertinism or total puritanism in the moral life. The aesthetic puzzle is whether the comic story and the Platonic kernel can be held together by Murdoch's archaic stance as an authorial will. And yet no other contemporary British novelist seems to me of Murdoch's eminence. Her formidable combination of intellectual drive and storytelling exuberance may never fuse into a great novel, but she has earned now the tribute she made to Jean Paul Sartre more than thirty years ago. She too has the style of the age.

IRIS MURDOCH

Against Dryness

The complaints which I wish to make are concerned primarily with prose, not with poetry, and primarily with novels, not with drama; and they are brief, simplified, abstract, and possibly insular. They are not to be construed as implying any precise picture of "the function of the writer." It is the function of the writer to write the best book he knows how to write. These remarks have to do with the background to present-day literature, in Liberal democracies in general and Welfare States in particular, in a sense in which this must be the concern of any serious critic.

We live in a scientific and anti-metaphysical age in which the dogmas, images, and precepts of religion have lost much of their power. We have not recovered from two wars and the experience of Hitler. We are also the heirs of the Enlightenment, Romanticism, and the Liberal tradition. These are the elements of our dilemma: whose chief feature, in my view, is that we have been left with far too shallow and flimsy an idea of human personality. I shall explain this.

Philosophy, like the newspapers, is both the guide and the mirror of its age. Let us look quickly at Anglo-Saxon philosophy and at French philosophy and see what picture of human personality we can gain from these two depositories of wisdom. Upon Anglo-Saxon philosophy the two most profound influences have been Hume and Kant: and it is not difficult to see in the current philosophical conception of the person the work of these two great thinkers. This conception consists in the joining of a materialistic behaviourism with a dramatic view of the individual as a solitary will. These

From *Encounter* 16, no. 1 (January 1961). © 1960/61 by *Encounter*, Ltd. Originally entitled "Against Dryness: A Polemical Sketch."

subtly give support to each other. From Hume through Bertrand Russell, with friendly help from mathematical logic and science, we derive the idea that reality is finally a quantity of material atoms and that significant discourse must relate itself directly or indirectly to reality so conceived. This position was most picturesquely summed up in Wittgenstein's *Tractatus*. Recent philosophy, especially the later work of Wittgenstein and the work of Gilbert Ryle derivative therefrom, alters this a little. The atomic Humian picture is abandoned in favour of a type of conceptual analysis (in many ways admirable) which emphasises the structural dependence of concepts upon the public language in which they are framed. This analysis has important results in the philosophy of mind, where it issues in modified behaviourism. Roughly: my inner life, for me just as for others, is identifiable as existing only through the application to it of public concepts, concepts which can only be constructed on the basis of overt behaviour.

This is one side of the picture, the Humian and post-Humian side. On the other side, we derive from Kant, and also Hobbes and Bentham through John Stuart Mill, a picture of the individual as a free rational will. With the removal of Kant's metaphysical background this individual is seen as alone. (He is in a certain sense alone in Kant's view also, that is: not confronted with real dissimilar others.) With the addition of some utilitarian optimism he is seen as eminently educable. With the addition of some modern psychology he is seen as capable of self-knowledge by methods agreeable to science and common sense. So we have the modern man, as he appears in many recent works on ethics and I believe also to a large extent in the popular consciousness.

We meet, for instance, a refined picture of this man in Stuart Hampshire's book *Thought and Action*. He is rational and totally free except in so far as, in the most ordinary lawcourt and commonsensical sense, his degree of self-awareness may vary. He is morally speaking monarch of all he surveys and totally responsible for his actions. Nothing transcends him. His moral language is a practical pointer, the instrument of his choices, the indication of his preferences. His inner life is resolved into his acts and choices, and his beliefs, which are also acts, since a belief can only be identified through its expression. His moral arguments are references to empirical facts backed up by decisions. The only moral word which he requires is "good" (or "right"), the word which expresses decision. His rationality expresses itself in awareness of the facts, whether about the world or about himself. The virtue which is fundamental to him is sincerity.

If we turn to French philosophy we may see, at least in that section of it which has most caught the popular imagination, I mean in the work of Jean Paul Sartre, essentially the same picture. It is interesting how extremely Kantian this picture is, for all Sartre's indebtedness to Hegelian sources. Again, the individual is pictured as solitary and totally free. There is no transcendent reality, there are no degrees of freedom. On the one hand there is the mass of psychological desires and social habits and prejudices, on the other hand there is the will. Certain dramas, more Hegelian in character, are of course enacted within the soul, but the isolation of the will remains. Hence *angoisse*. Hence, too, the special anti-bourgeois flavour of Sartre's philosophy which makes it appeal to many intellectuals: the ordinary traditional picture of personality and the virtues lies under suspicion of *mauvaise foi*. Again the only real virtue is sincerity. It is, I think, no accident that, however much philosophical and other criticism Sartre may receive, this powerful picture has caught our imagination. The Marxist critics may plausibly claim that it represents the essence of the Liberal theory of personality.

It will be pointed out that other phenomenological theories (leaving aside Marxism) have attempted to do what Sartre has failed to do, and that there are notable philosophers who have offered a different picture of the soul. Yes; yet from my own knowledge of the scene I would doubt whether any (non-Marxist) account of human personality has yet emerged from phenomenology which is fundamentally unlike the one which I have described and can vie with it in imaginative power. It may be said that philosophy cannot in fact produce such an account. I am not sure about this, nor is this large question my concern here. I express merely my belief that, for the Liberal world, philosophy is not in fact at present able to offer us any other complete and powerful picture of the soul. I return now to England and the Anglo-Saxon tradition.

The welfare state has come about as a result, largely, of socialist thinking and socialist endeavour. It has seemed to bring a certain struggle to an end; and with that ending has come a lassitude about fundamentals. If we compare the language of the original Labour Party constitution with that of its recent successor we see an impoverishment of thinking and language which is typical. The Welfare State is the reward of "empiricism in politics." It has represented to us a set of thoroughly desirable but limited ends, which could be conceived *in non-theoretical terms*; and in pursuing it, in allowing the idea of it to dominate the more naturally theoretical wing of our political scene, we have to a large extent lost our theories. Our central conception is still a debilitated form of Mill's equation: happiness equals freedom equals personality. There should have been a revolt against utilitarianism, but for many reasons it has not taken place. In 1905 John Maynard Keynes and his friends welcomed the philosophy of G. E. Moore because Moore reinstated the concept of experience, Moore directed attention away from the mechanics of action and towards the inner life. But Moore's "experience" was too shallow a concept; and a scientific age with simple attainable empirical aims has preferred a more behaviouristic philosophy.

What have we lost here? And what have we perhaps never had? We have suffered a general loss of concepts, the loss of a moral and political vocabulary. We no longer use a spread-out substantial picture of the manifold virtues of man and society. We no longer see man against a background of values, of realities, which transcend him. We picture man as a brave naked will surrounded by an easily comprehended empirical world. For the hard idea of truth we have substituted a facile idea of sincerity. What we have never had, of course, is a satisfactory Liberal theory of personality, a theory of man as free and separate and related to a rich and complicated world from which, as a moral being, he has much to learn. We have bought the Liberal theory as it stands, because we have wished to encourage people to think of themselves as free, at the cost of surrendering the background.

We have never solved the problems about human personality posed by the Enlightenment. Between the various concepts available to us the real question has escaped: and now, in a curious way, our present situation is analogous to an 18th-century one. We retain a rationalistic optimism about the beneficent results of education, or rather technology. We combine this with a romantic conception of "the human condition," a picture of the individual as stripped and solitary: a conception which has, since Hitler, gained a peculiar intensity.

The 18th century was an era of rationalistic allegories and moral tales. The 19th century (roughly) was the great era of the novel; and the novel throve upon a dynamic merging of the idea of person with the idea of class. Because 19th-century society was dynamic and interesting and because (to use a Marxist notion) the type and the individual could there be seen as merged, the solution of the 18th-century problem could be put off. It has been put off till now. Now that the structure of society is less interesting and less alive than it was in the 19th century, and now that Welfare economics have removed certain incentives to thinking, and now that the values of science are so much taken for granted, we confront in a particularly dark and confusing form a dilemma which has been with us implicitly since the Enlightenment, or since the beginning, wherever exactly one wishes to place it, of the modern Liberal world.

If we consider 20th-century literature as compared with 19th-century literature, we notice certain significant contrasts. I said that, in a way, we were back in the 18th century, the era of rationalistic allegories and moral tales, the era when the idea of human nature was unitary and single. The 19th-century novel (I use these terms boldly and roughly: of course there were exceptions) was not concerned with "the human condition," it was concerned with real various individuals struggling in society. The 20th-century novel is usually either crystalline or journalistic; that is, it is either a small quasi-allegorical object portraying the human condition and not containing "characters" in the 19th-century sense, or else it is a large shape-less quasi-documentary object, the degenerate descendant of the 19th-century novel, telling, with pale conventional characters, some straightforward story enlivened with empirical facts. Neither of these kinds of literature engages with the problem that I mentioned above.

It may readily be noted that if our prose fiction is either crystalline or journalistic, the crystalline works are usually the better ones. They are what the more serious writers want to create. We may recall the ideal of "dryness" which we associate with the symbolist movement, with writers such as T. E. Hulme and T. S. Eliot, with Paul Valery, with Wittgenstein. This "dryness" (smallness, clearness, self-containedness) is a nemesis of Roman-ticism. Indeed it *is* Romanticism in a later phase. The pure, clean, self-contained "symbol," the exemplar incidentally of what Kant, ancestor of both Liberalism and Romanticism, required art to be, is the analogue of the lonely self-contained individual. It is what is left of the otherworldliness of Romanticism when the "messy" humanitarian and revolutionary elements have spent their force. The temptation of art, a temptation to which every work of art yields except the greatest ones, is to console. The modern writer, frightened of technology and (in England) abandoned by philosophy and (in France) presented with simplified dramatic theories, attempts to console us by myths or by stories.

On the whole: his truth is sincerity and his imagination is fantasy. Fantasy operates either with shapeless daydreams (the journalistic story) or with small myths, toys, crystals. Each in his own way produces a sort of "dream necessity." Neither grapples with reality: hence "fantasy," not "imagination."

The proper home of the symbol, in the "symbolist" sense, is poetry. Even there it may play an equivocal role since there is something in sym-bolism which is inimical to words, out of which, we have been reminded, poems are constructed. Certainly the invasion of other areas by what I may call, for short, "symbolist ideals," has helped to bring about a decline of prose. Eloquence is out of fashion; even "style," except in a very austere sense of this term, is out of fashion.

T. S. Eliot and Jean Paul Sartre, dissimilar enough as thinkers, both tend to undervalue prose and to deny it any *imaginative* function. Poetry is the creation of linguistic quasi-things; prose is for explanation and exposition, it is essentially didactic, documentary, informative. Prose is ideally transparent; it is only *faute de mieux* written in words. The influential modern stylist is Hemingway. It would be almost inconceivable now to write like Landor. Most modern English novels indeed are not *written*. One feels they could slip into some other medium without much loss. It takes a foreigner like Nabokov or an Irishman like Beckett to animate prose language into an imaginative stuff in its own right.

Tolstoy who said that art was an expression of the religious perception of the age was nearer the truth than Kant who saw it as the imagination in a frolic with the understanding. The connection between art and the moral life has languished because we are losing our sense of form and structure in the moral world itself. Linguistic and existentialist behaviourism, our Romantic philosophy, has reduced our vocabulary and simplified and impoverished our view of the inner life. It is natural that a Liberal democratic society will not be concerned with techniques of improvement, will deny that virtue is knowledge, will emphasise choice at the expense of vision; and a Welfare State will weaken the incentives to investigate the bases of a Liberal democratic society. For political purposes we have been encouraged to think of ourselves as totally free and responsible, knowing everything we need to know for the important purposes of life. But this is one of the things of which Hume said that it may be true in politics but false in fact; and is it really true in politics? We need a post-Kantian unromantic Liberalism with a different image of freedom.

The technique of becoming free is more difficult than John Stuart Mill imagined. We need more concepts than our philosophies have furnished us with. We need to be enabled to think in terms of degrees of freedom, and to picture, in a nonmetaphysical, nontotalitarian, and nonreligious sense, the transcendence of reality. A simpleminded faith in science, together with the assumption that we are all rational and totally free, engenders a dangerous lack of curiosity about the real world, a failure to appreciate the difficulties of knowing it. We need to return from the self-centred concept of sincerity to the other-centred concept of truth. We are not isolated free choosers, monarchs of all we survey but benighted creatures sunk in a reality whose nature we are constantly and overwhelmingly tempted to deform by fantasy. Our current picture of freedom encourages a dreamlike facility; whereas what we require is a renewed sense of the difficulty and complexity of the moral life and the opacity of persons. We need more concepts in terms of which

to picture the substance of our being; it is through an enriching and deep-
ening of concepts that moral progress takes place. Simone Weil said that
morality was a matter of attention not of will. We need a new vocabulary
of attention.

It is here that literature is so important, especially since it has taken
over some of the tasks formerly performed by philosophy. Through literature
we can rediscover a sense of the density of our lives. Literature can arm us
against consolation and fantasy and can help us to recover from the ailments
of Romanticism. If it can be said to have a task, now, that surely is its task.
But if it is to perform it, prose must recover its former glory, eloquence
and discourse must return. I would connect eloquence with the attempt to
speak the truth. I think here of the work of Albert Camus. All his novels
were *written*, but the last one, though less striking and successful than the
first two, seems to me to have been a more serious attempt upon the truth
and illustrates what I mean by eloquence.

It is curious that modern literature, which is so much concerned with
violence, contains so few convincing pictures of evil.

Our inability to imagine evil is a consequence of the facile, dramatic
and, in spite of Hitler, optimistic picture of ourselves with which we work.
Our difficulty about form, about images—our tendency to produce works
which are either crystalline or journalistic—is a symptom of our situation.
Form itself can be a temptation, making the work of art into a small myth
which is a self-contained and indeed self-satisfied individual. We need to
turn our attention away from the consoling dream necessity of Romanticism,
away from the dry symbol, the bogus individual, the false whole, towards
the real impenetrable human person. That this person is substantial, impenetrable, individual, indefinable, and valuable is after all the fundamental
tenet of Liberalism.

It is here, however much one may criticise the emptiness of the Liberal
idea of freedom, however much one may talk in terms of restoring a lost
unity, that one is forever at odds with Marxism. Reality is not a given
whole. An understanding of this, a respect for the contingent, is essential
to imagination as opposed to fantasy. Our sense of form, which is an aspect
of our desire for consolation, can be a danger to our sense of reality as a rich
receding background. Against the consolations of form, the clean crystalline
work, the simplified fantasy-myth, we must pit the destructive power of
the now so unfashionable naturalistic idea of character.

Real people are destructive of myth, contingency is destructive of fantasy and opens the way for imagination. Think of the Russians, those great
masters of the contingent. Too much contingency of course may turn art

into journalism. But since reality is incomplete, art must not be too much afraid of incompleteness. Literature must always represent a battle between real people and images; and what it requires now is a much stronger and more complex conception of the former.

In morals and politics we have stripped ourselves of concepts. Literature, in curing its own ills, can give us a new vocabulary of experience, and a truer picture of freedom. With this, renewing our sense of distance, we may remind ourselves that art too lives in a region where all human endeavour is failure. Perhaps only Shakespeare manages to create at the highest level both images and people; and even *Hamlet* looks second-rate compared with *Lear*. Only the very greatest art invigorates without consoling, and defeats our attempts, in W. H. Auden's words, to use it as magic.

FREDERICK J. HOFFMAN

The Italian Girl

I have elsewhere discussed seven of Miss Murdoch's novels (*Critique*, Spring, 1964); I should like here to discuss the most recent, *The Italian Girl* (1964), in terms of her past career, and to assess its place in the scheme of things. It has not had a popular success; in fact, critics have complained of its not having "come to anything," of its having shifted too quickly from one incident to another, of its being, in the end, "empty and without substance." From an orthodox critical point of view, these objections may be valid; but there is no reason to assume that criticism of this novel needs to remain "orthodox."

It is my contention that *The Italian Girl* is an exemplary work, illustrating beautifully Miss Murdoch's definition of "love" and "the idea of perfection" in her 1964 *Yale Review* essay. The people in it are seen in a remarkable variety of attitudes, each of them "gathered in" by the narrator, Edmund Narraway. His function is only partly to see what is going on and to assess it; eventually he too becomes involved in the action. In short, he both appraises the action and serves to push it forward; or, to put it another way, the narrator's original disposition is neither strong nor inflexible enough for him simply to stand on the edge of events and to give them an uncompromising evaluation.

To begin with, Narraway appears for the funeral of his mother; and his judgment of her is a mixture of distaste and horror: "Her dead face had an expression which I had known upon it in life, a sort of soft crazed expression, like a Grünewald Saint Anthony, a look of elated madness and

From *Shenandoah: The Washington and Lee Review* 17, no. 1 (Autumn 1965). © 1965 by Washington and Lee University. Originally entitled "The Miracle of Contingency: The Novels of Iris Murdoch."

suffering." Mortality and madness, here combined in the face in the coffin, set the tone of the novel's progress, as the narrator proceeds to examine every characteristic human gesture. *The Italian Girl* does not have a "plot" that might satisfy any person who seeks only the pleasure of motion in his reading. The events are, instead, strangely mixed, and even jumbled; and the major effects are those involved in a "straightening out" of human relations. At the beginning the novel's tone seems to take off from the face in the coffin: she "had got inside me, [the narrator says of his dead mother] into the depths of my being, there was no abyss and no darkness where she was not."

The ideally suitable event in Miss Murdoch's judgment as a philosopher is that in which one person's view of another is slowly and appropriately changed. The change comes after a slow meditation over what one person morally owes to another; this is what she has called the effect of love upon human relationships. Narraway begins by hating his mother, or by bringing his hatred of her to her funeral. He ends by making awkward gestures of love toward several beings. That these are comical and even absurd does not denigrate them necessarily. In short, he starts off with fixed though narrow preconceptions, and he tries, not without some success, to become another kind of person before the story is finally put away.

There are several indications of change: from coffin to monument; from innocence to evil; from love as a pose, to love as an awkward but sincere expression of feeling. Each of these marks a great effort of the imagination and will. The criticism basic to all of these is directed against the inappropriateness of a Christian pose that is too abstract to account for the "reality of persons."

> I wished, not for the first time, that I had been brought up as
> a Christian. Christianity was not inside me, for all that I some-
> times aped it, and I knew the loss to be terrible.

Narraway's worst fault is an inverted "elegance"; confusion and muddles and "personal smells" are detestable to him; his distaste for them seems a priori and not deserved. He needs to be inducted into both facts and fragments of human experience. The apparent "jumble" of much of the novel is a consequence of his desperate attempt to take in and understand any number of human evidences which he has begun by detesting and ends by accepting. The atmosphere of the crematorium gives way to that of the workshop of Narraway's brother, Otto, a place where he carves epitaphs in monumental stone. Edmund describes it as "labyrinth, his metaphysical torture chamber." But the progress is away from death, toward life, and from hatred to love—however imperfect the evidences of both happen to be.

Miss Murdoch believes that both "life" and "love" must be taken patiently, as imperfect human conditions, which only the kind of "meditation" that she describes in her more recent *Yale Review* essay can help one to accept. So there are much confusion, unhappiness, and untidiness as Edmund moves toward a condition of acceptance. He is frequently shocked by what human beings will do to violate the decorums he has grown to respect. He must, eventually, reject these decorums, or go mad with the shock and the surprise of his discoveries about human beings.

Two other characters testify to Miss Murdoch's habit of "sudden abundance." The two Levkins, from Russia, are both slightly mad, and in any case abnormally greedy for experience; they provided a curious sense of opposition to the members of Edmund's family. They are primarily the Evil that invades Innocence; and Narraway, in his attempts to understand them, makes them appear more troublesome and confusing than they actually are. Prevailing over all scenes of human aberrance is the Italian girl of the title, with "an unsmiling, impersonal reticence," a "grave, demanding face, [an] anonymous black dress, [a] trailing bun of hair." Edmund must be introduced to life and love; life is just not all "monks and mess," as Isabel says of Edmund's view of it. He must be helped to discover otherwise. The experience is bound to prove awkward. Edmund is "tempted," after having been entirely disgusted by the *schwärmerei* of human obscenities; he very clumsily experiments with sex, and the situation—comic throughout—gradually changes as Edmund adjusts to it.

> As it was, [Isabel] simply radiated these obscure frenzied little waves of sexual need and would-be authority which, although I was strictly indifferent to them, did have a generally disturbing effect.

The narrator's experience stands, roughly, eccentrically, and idiosyncratically, for the "stuff of life." It is not a condition which he is proud to see, but he does come to realize that it is necessary for him to see it. The comedy as well as the humanity is that he is shocked by everything that everyone else takes for granted, or at least as remediable. The changes occur when it is noted that he is not merely "scandalized" by a human event but is also emotionally stirred by it. Some of the incidents *are* astonishing and even grotesque. But they are all a part of his education, and the change of tone from the novel's beginning to its end is the form of human "meditation" that Miss Murdoch hopes to enforce through her treatment of the shocking "reality of persons." In the end, those persons who have survived are matured: "we all died for a moment [Edmund says], but then what came after had a greater certainty."

The value of this novel depends upon its narrator, expecially upon his growth from naïveté to the greater sophistication and understanding of the novel's conclusion. On the surface, there are confusion, distortion, and a general mangling of the human scene. Perhaps Miss Murdoch takes too much pleasure in the mêlée; but there is no question that she intends the changes to be meaningful, in the sense that her observations on "The Idea of Perfection" are pertinent.

I should say, by way of conclusion, that philosophy and art never exactly touch or converge in Miss Murdoch's work. This is partly because the two disciplines remain adamantly apart, and have quite different tones. But she is also responsible for a "feminine" view of philosophy. She says, in many ways, to her masculine colleagues: let's have done with this abstracting nonsense and see how human beings do, after all, torture one another; perhaps if we do, we can see eventually how they may come to *love* one another.

FRANK KERMODE

Bruno's Dream

There are middle-aged men, fat and bald or both, content with their wives or mistresses or gentle perversities, to whom appears, disposing them in various postures of prayer and pain, the lord of terrible aspect. Perhaps love strikes them in their civilized but dirty houses looking out over Lots Road Power Station, or as they stroll in the Brompton Cemetery. In one such house lives a very old, slowly dying man, drinking champagne, reading books about spiders, handling his valuable stamp collection, or thinking of his life and meditating the possibility of forgiveness by the dead. Outside, the rain beats incessantly on the windows, the Thames threatens an Old Testament flood. In another part of the house this man's widowed son-in-law is in bed with the maid, who is named Adelaide de Crecy, and who drops only the best Wedgwood, on purpose. Observing them is a thin black mystic called Nigel, whom we in turn are to observe in the most bizarre situations—for example, tying up his sleeping twin with an ingenious machine. There is a constant interest in resemblances. There are many judgements and some slaughters, though none is either accidental or casual. The pubs of Chelsea are catalogued, the operations of a printing press described. A brief manual of arachnology is deftly divided and served to us in whispers. There is a Thames-side duel, the flood happens. People die in aeroplanes, of cancer, by drowning. They are printers, civil servants, male nurses, probation officers, and the like, just the kind of people you'd expect all this sort of thing to happen to. Of course it's all made up, and if the question should be, by whom? the foregoing fantasy is an authoritative leak.

From *Modern Essays*. © 1970 by Frank Kermode. Collins/Fontana Books, 1971. Originally entitled "Iris Murdoch."

The point is simply this, that the taste of a Murdoch novel is instantly recognized, if not easily described; and despite the efficiency of her prose— very professional, very direct, though allowing for a lot to go on under the surface—this taste is somehow a bit high. Served so frequently with dishes of this kind, the diner may become fuddled or cantankerous, or he may grow, on the other hand, addicted so that Miss Murdoch's annual novel is hailed antiphonally by peevish dyspeptics who are having to give her up and gourmets who call it her best so far. To anyone trying to decide which half of the chorus to join, there is another difficulty, and it is that Miss Murdoch, seconded by Mr. Bayley in his critical works, has expressed deeply pondered and very interesting views on what novels ought to be, and these views are difficult to reconcile with the novels she herself writes. As to this new novel, it may very well be her best, it may cause defections and certainly it raises all the problems very acutely.

Miss Murdoch has often said that art, in so far as it has to deal in shapes and forms, and not in the discontinuities and irrelevances of common perception and experience, can be a false consolation to us but that great art is distinguished by not being that. It is a theme of the present book. She is convinced, as she once remarked to me in an uneasy television discussion, that a writer can succumb to the pattern of his book, and so destroy the freedom of his characters for the sake of some comforting, fraudulent design. Most people (everybody except very good people) choose roles, and are in some measure diminished though comforted by them; and if a novelist reduces his people in the same way, and makes them subserve some comforting purpose of his own, he is not allowing them to be what people might and should be: baffling, impenetrable, mysterious. The power to make the necessary connections without reducing the essential mystery is, simply, love, whether in personal relations or in fiction. It is quite legitimate, here, to think of Forster; if the best self of Bloomsbury has an heir, it is Miss Murdoch.

But the preferred model is, as we all know, Tolstoy. And Miss Murdoch is extremely unlike Tolstoy. She adores patterns and plots, and there is not the slightest sign that anyone resembling Natasha or Anna, Vronsky or Pierre, will ever comply with them. She is, rather, a one-woman *commedia dell'arte*; given a *soggetto*, she will produce the most ingeniously developed performance. But here the difficulty occurs: in doing so she will have in mind many deep speculations about fiction and reality, about ethics, about language, about many other things. They will only very occasionally affect the surface of her story; some of the characteristic pleasure derives from the sense that a lot is going on down below. There, something difficult is being said, or some myth or ritual is being secretly enacted.

This isn't to say that Miss Murdoch succumbs to her pattern; in this book anyway she does not. Perhaps the denouement, which is both unexpected and apt, as Aristotle wished, surprised even her. But this enhances the feeling that these amorous collisions are a sort of war game, it moves obscured by a plausible mist of contingent detail. In this *Bruno's Dream* resembles, of course, many of her earlier books. There is, one feels, a basic game with the unstated rules of which these books in their different ways comply. Contingency is conscripted (people meet or see each other very conveniently: in the last novel the author was comically cavalier about this, and made a husband and wife die simultaneously of double pneumonia, affecting one lung apiece, perhaps). Why is the biographical detail handled with such farcical briskness? Because there is no time to be lost in getting everybody thrown into the great centrifuge of love; because there are to hand squads of significant detail, of easy, surprising, symbol-concealing dialogue. All this interests Miss Murdoch more than most people. It leads us, if we can follow down to the rite or formula which the book is half-hiding. Not that all is concealment; there is sometimes a suspicious candour. The power station and the cemetery are very large symbols of love and death. There is a purple passage about the mystical young man Nigel who thinks he is God, or a god, with puns on Omphalos, Om and phallos. There are meditations, sometimes direct, sometimes oblique, on Last Things, on the necessary and the contingent, on time as we experience it in dying and in reading novels, on ritual as a means of reversing the flow of time. If, in the end, we are consoled, rather than made to think on these things, we are, on the Murdoch view, either contingent persons, or we are dealing only with a minor work of art.

Well, she makes us say things like that, but we should also say that the pleasures she offers are unique and potent. One of them may well be that each novel contains somewhere the ghost of a major novel. This one, for example, Bruno, perhaps a Dantesque name, is at the point where the three dreams cross, past, present, future, the dreams of the dying man and the novelist have to fake into a continuum. Bruno is a Tithonus figure; he ages while the women in his life, because they are dead, do not. In his waking dream he tries to "propriate" (propitiate?) their shades. Defeated by his father, he is a failed zoologist, a failed philatelist, a failed husband; everything he started shrank in size before he finished it, even his one love affair. Will his estranged son forgive him, enact a ritual of reconciliation? Is he repenting the right things? The omniscient, philosophic, epigrammatic author remarks that "we regret only the frailty which the form of our life has made us own to." For Bruno, for most, a present selects its past.

People are either necessary or contingent. Bruno's hedonist son-in-law

Danby is contingent, at first anyway. Later the god strikes him into necessity for a while. The dreadful mystic Nigel, a symbol of some sort of god—peering through bedroom windows, telling tales—is, in his ecstasy, an image of the light beyond perception ("tithonic," it used to be called), a channel for such light, a "lazar" (laser?) beam, a dancer who enacts the circular and reciprocal motions of the angels of love and death, which are finally one. (In working hours he is Bruno's nurse.) It is Bruno's desire to be reconciled with his son, Miles, who years before upset him by marrying an Indian girl called Parvati, that starts the plot. Miles is a poet, happily married to a second, more contingent wife, and giving houseroom to a plain, necessary sister-in-law, when both he and his brother-in-law (abandoning one the wife and the other the maidservant) are struck down by love for the sister-in-law Lisa, who has a First in Greats, has joined and left the Poor Clares, and is an East End schoolmistress and unpaid probation officer. Miles loses but comes to terms with the death of Parvati and so can write good poems. Danby gets the sister-in-law; the rejected Adelaide gets Nigel's twin, who fights a duel with Danby, organized for divine kicks by Nigel. There is a flood. Miles's wife is happy with 90-year-old Bruno. All the time it rains like hell, on the town and in the hearts, and indeed the eyes, of the characters. The valuable stamps are lost, the housefly man and the spider God are alike manipulated, and considered; Bruno fades into non-time, accompanied by love, and we reach an unexpected but still consoling end.

Hopeless love showed Miles how to face Parvati's death, and allowed his god to come. Does the novel make death poetic, as Miles's early, bad, poem did? The novel examines itself on this. If Miles is right, we learn, the power to deal with necessity, summon the god and reverse time without lying, depends upon self-abnegation, a way of seeing love as death. Nigel, indeed, says the same thing; but Miles is unlovable, Nigel phoney. Or so they seem to me, but then Miss Murdoch's necessary people often do. It is they who can find God in spiders, as well as in poems, in bed, and in death. At this level she is not writing for "contingent persons," which most of her readers necessarily are. They seek, like Bruno, a consoling magic, a pleasing peripeteia, in life, perhaps in death; and they find it in Miss Murdoch's plots, not in her subtexts.

Nevertheless these subjects touch the nerves that great fiction assaults. The treatment of time in this book, occasionally breaking the surface in fragmentary philosophical allusion, is exceedingly rich and various, involving ritual and eschatology, but also penetrating the language: there is a casual linguistic insistence on the way in which our bodies are extended in space, our minds in time, on the ritual quality of momentary gestures, whether of men or spiders. These are the time and the space from which only the god can release us, whether as love or death. For the dying and for lovers there are no things just one after another, only last things: so death, love, and their instruments, myth and fiction, undo the work of time. But not by lying.

The reality in which they deal is a different reality from the order of ordinary poetry, as Miles (who alone of the characters lives in a clean, well-lighted place) has to learn. The contingent must be got in; it can be the smell, the spotted hands, of an aged man. Diana, the self-interested hedonist unexpectedly paired with Bruno, asks: "Is this not the most pointless of all loves? Like loving death itself." This reality is a difficult vocation. One can recognize that without being irresistibly drawn.

So, perhaps, with Miss Murdoch, who not only makes her sacral patterns but expresses herself, as some of her characters do, in terms of a self-interested hedonism; I mean that her rituals are hazed over by pleasure, by a love which, to the best of its ability, ostracizes death. But this book tries to get it in. What, in the end, is most beautiful about it is that we never think of these old and aging people, tortured by love and death, as absurd. The nearer they are to death, the more just and imperative their loves. Only at the point of death is the point of love fully evident; necessary persons, we gather, know that in the death of the desiring body love achieves being.

Well, that is to say too much, and say it wrongly. The book is full of delicate and unobtrusive mysteries. It is also, at all levels, arbitrarily amusing, gaily and seriously intelligent, disappointing only by the fantastically high standards it contrives to suggest. And a review which leaves most of that out should end with a simple expression of gratitude.

FRANK BALDANZA

The Nice and the Good

"*The Nice and the Good* is a pretty open one, I think—perhaps the most open one I've done yet," Miss Murdoch remarked in an interview with W. K. Rose (for *London Magazine* 1968). This openness, which involves "more accidental and separate and free characters," constitutes her deepest aim both as a practicing novelist and as a theorist, although, as many critics have pointed out, her natural talents incline her toward the "closed," tightly patterned, neatly arranged little myth, as in *A Severed Head*. But the openness is not just a matter of characters; *The Nice and the Good* is looser in structure than many another of her works, and is probably her longest book to date. And in the success of its openness, it is crammed with casual little gems, sometimes sparkling within the context, as in Dickens, with little relevance to an overall pattern, but thoroughly delightful in themselves. For example, a fatuously self-satisfied matron visits the home of her Platonic lover in order to have a look at his shaggy-sexy chauffeur when she knows the master is out; the accident of dropping a glove into the disposal in the kitchen sink concentrates all kinds of ambient sexual electricity between the two, eventuating in a soulful kiss as they consume the slivovitz and *marrons glacés* which were the gift-pretext for her visit.

This structural openness, however, is obviously gained at the cost of greater diffusion and lack of concentration, so it is especially important to note the thematic emphases of this work in whose interest the openness was attained.

At one point late in *Absalom, Absalom!* Quentin and Shreve, the two

From *Modern Fiction Studies* 15, no. 3 (Autumn 1969). © 1969 by Purdue Research Foundation, West Lafayette, Ind.

youthful speculators, declare that they have investigated all other aspects of Thomas Sutpen's family history, and now it is time to talk about love, which they consider the last and greatest of concerns. Miss Murdoch is at the same point in her own career. While she has for a long time insisted that love is her primary subject, she says in her interview with Mr. Rose that she was more strongly preoccupied in her earlier works with freedom; now, however, "what I am concerned about really is love." This is a kind of love that grows out of sex, and transcends it without, however, abolishing it in the process. If brute sex, as she admits, leads to the fairly mechanical round of couplings that distinguished many of the closed novels like *A Severed Head*, then the open novel has this aim:

> sex is a very great mystifier, it's a very great dark force. It makes us do all kinds of things we don't understand and very often don't want to do. The kind of opening out of love as a world where we really can see other people and are not simply dominated by our own slavish impulses and obsessions, this is something which I would want very much to explore and which I think is very difficult. All these demons and so on are connected with the obsessional side of one's life, which in a sense has got to be overcome.

In fact, the overcoming of demons is a general movement in this novel [*The Nice and the Good*] on the part of the sympathetic characters; we shall note later on how the conquering of demons thus gives this work a movement in the direction opposite to that of the characters in *The Time of the Angels*, who succumb to these gaseous emanations.

The most intense focus for the conquering of obsessive demons is the flawed, culpable, questing-learning male, who is so abundant in the author's earlier works—in this case John Ducane, assigned by his superior at Whitehall to investigate the suicide of a bureaucrat who is involved in occultism tinged with seedy sexual goings-on that distinctly recall the celebrated Profumo scandal. He also serves as a father-confessor and advisor to a crowded cast of "accidental and separate and free" characters, largely located at Trescombe, the Victorian Gothic seaside country home of John's superior Octavian Gray. Among the personages are Barbara, the Gray daughter; two lonely women—Paula Biranne, a divorcée with twins and Mary Clothier, a widow with an adolescent son—and two eccentric bachelors—Willy Kost, a melancholic refugee scholar and Theodore, Octavian's brother, an engineer who left India under a cloud (thus recalling Humphrey Finch of *An Unofficial Rose*, who was drummed out of the service in Marrakech for a similar homosexual involvement).

The trajectory of the plot is a forked one, as it were, with the double paths overlapping toward the end; the plot was obviously not planned in advance in the same kind of detail as in a closed novel like *The Italian Girl* or *A Severed Head*, but the general air of improvisation is now and then overlaid by Miss Murdoch's inveterate tendency toward the neat tying up of loose ends. One of the paths of the trajectory is the solution of the Radeechy suicide, which really holds no surprises—it turns out to have been just about the kind of suicide that surface appearances indicated, although the quest involves the exposure of many shoddy activities and the solution of an occultist acrostic; and it provides much moral anxiety for John Ducane in his belated process of growing up.

The second trajectory is the fundamental pairing off of partners at the end of the work, accomplished in this case with thematic twists and flairs appropriate to the particular thesis about love that we have just quoted. At one end of the age continuum, Octavian and Kate Gray remain in their static marital relationship, and at the other end, Pierce Clothier and Barbara Gray find their physical sexual maturity in a wickedly witty scene of first intercourse:

> "Was that really it?"
> "Yes."
> "Are you sure you did it right?"
> "My God, I'm sure!"
> "Well, I don't like it."
> "Girls never do the first time."
> "Perhaps I'm a Lesbian."

For the rest, all the pairings, which we shall hereafter survey in greater detail, are between divorced, widowed, and otherwise experienced partners who are learning to live with past mistakes in the process of discovering more fully the nature of love as real contact with real other persons.

The bridges between the two themes are many, in an implied sense, since the Radeechy suicide mystery occurs at Octavian Gray's office, and the marital couplings largely center around his home, with the flotsam and jetsam of blackmailing and opportunistic servants as a buffer zone between the two. The firmest tie between the two areas is John Ducane who is conducting a mock affair with Kate Gray in his off moments from the suicide investigation. A parallel tie consists of the divorced Biranne couple, Richard being the only living survivor of the Radeechy imbroglio; and since Paula and the twins have been living at Trescombe, her reconciliation with Richard at the end of the book spans the office-home dichotomy.

The novel is haunted by several ghosts, in the sense that great swatches of material recall earlier characters, situations, plots, ideas, and themes from Miss Murdoch's own novels; and in the sense that there are manifold recalls of the ambience of several other novelists. Edward and Henrietta, the Birannes' nine-year-old twins, for example, strongly resemble Julius and Dora Calderon of Ivy Compton-Burnett's *Elders and Betters*, as did Felicity Mor of *The Sandcastle*. Although their sightings of flying saucers give them a twist of contemporaneity inconceivable in a work of Miss Compton-Burnett, they seem to owe to her their fiendishly clever intelligence, their secret cultic games, and the fierce exclusivity of their mutual league against adult intrusion. Although the adolescents, Pierce and Barbara, may also owe a little to Miss Compton-Burnett, Barbara's closest forbear is Annette Cockayne of *The Flight from the Enchanter*, this time in a less hectic manifestation.

But the most haunting resemblances are to the works of Muriel Spark, and particularly to *The Bachelors*. In the course of Miss Murdoch's novel, the moral substance of the theme fines itself down inexorably to the confrontation between the investigator, John Ducane, and the morally culpable accessory to the murder of Claudia Radeechy and the suicide of her husband, Richard Biranne, who was on the fringe of Radeechy's spiritualistic and black-magic rituals. In much the same way, *The Bachelors* is ordered around the confrontation of the handwriting expert Ronald Bridges and the occultist-Lothario-charlatan Patrick Seaton in the climactic trial scene of that novel. And just as Ronald's coming to terms with his mistaken priestly vocation is intimately tied in with what he learns in this investigation, so is John Ducane's moral development gauged by the course of his search, although *his* priestly inclinations are a matter of vicarious—but definite—secular roles as confessor and advisor to friends.

The major difference between the two investigations is that while Ronald testifies in a court of law which sentences Patrick to a term in prison, John Ducane consciously eschews legal prosecution by exacting retribution for Biranne's moral failings in his own drawing room, stipulating a reconciliation with Paula as Richard's main "sentence"—one obviously conceived not as punishment but as a kind of creative, therapeutic discipline in encountering the reality of other persons.

This decision came about as a result of John's earlier moral epiphany when, nearly certain to drown in an effort to save the suicide-bent Pierce Clothier (his future stepson, although he does not know it at the time) from an undersea grotto, he has the following vision. He and Pierce are desperately waiting for the tide to retreat as they lie together forced into tense contact, with a dog between them, having wriggled into the same vest in an effort to combat the extreme cold:

I wonder if this is the end, thought Ducane, and if so what it will all have amounted to. How tawdry and small it has all been. He saw himself now as a little rat, a busy little scurrying rat, seeking out its own little advantages and comforts. To live easily, to have cosy familiar pleasures, to be well thought of. . . . The coloured images were returning now to his closed eyes. He saw the face of Biranne near to him, as in a silent film, moving, mouthing, but unheard. He thought, if I ever get out of here I will be no man's judge. Nothing is worth doing except to kill the little rat, not to judge, not to be superior, not to exercise power, not to seek, seek, seek. To love and to reconcile and to forgive, only this matters. All power is sin and all law is frailty. Love is the only justice. Forgiveness, reconciliation, not law.

While there are several wry references to John's assumption of the role of God to enforce a kind of private moral blackmail, Miss Murdoch obviously chose this private form of justice because, in striking contrast to the over-whelming triumph of virulent evil in *The Time of the Angels*, she meant in this work to represent evil in a lesser role. While we must be wary of quoting any one speech as authoritative for the author, two such pronouncements in this novel can hardly be accidental in placing evil in its proper context. In one case Willy Kost is trying to persuade John's former mistress, Jessica, to renounce her venomous jealousy and possessiveness; he says all humans are caught in a network of formerly enacted evil:

"We are not good people, Jessica, and we shall always be involved in that great network, you and I. All we can do is constantly to notice when we begin to act badly, to check ourselves, to go back, to coax our weakness and inspire our strength, to call upon the names of virtues of which we know perhaps only the names. We are not good people, and the best we can hope for is to be gentle, to forgive each other and to forgive the past, to be forgiven ourselves and to accept this forgiveness, and to return again to the beautiful unexpected strangeness of the world."

And at the very end of the novel, as if Willy had forgotten this wisdom, he is droning away in an anguished confession to Theo about his betrayals of comrades at Dachau, when Theo, fussing with tea in the kitchen, meditates:

He thought, what is the point here, what is the point. What can I say to him? That one must soon forget one's sins in the claims of others. But how to forget. The point is that nothing matters except loving what is good. Not to look at evil but to look at good. Only this contemplation breaks the tyranny of the past, breaks the adherence of evil to the personality, breaks, in the end, the personality itself. In the light of the good, evil can be seen in its place, not owned, just existing, in its place.

We might incidentally note in passing that John's vision of himself reveals a subsidiary theme, a preoccupation with personal comfort, imaged as a rat that needs to be killed; Theo approaches a similar theme in his assertion that breaking adherence of evil to the personality will eventually break the personality itself, which he conceives of as the same kind of rat of personal indulgence: "I am sunk in the wreck of myself. . . . I live in myself like a mouse inside a ruin. I am huge, sprawling, corrupt, and empty. The mouse moves, the ruin moulders. That is all." In the closing pages of the novel, we learn that Theo left India because he had attempted to seduce a novice in the Buddhist monastery where he was studying, and when the boy committed suicide, Theo fled. In his vow to return to the monastery now in his old age, he discovers there is a kind of love superior to the "seek, seek, seek" kind mentioned by John (and which bears a resemblance to the similarly phrased idea in Bellow's *Henderson the Rain King*), and he gives a benediction to the title of the book:

> Theo had begun to glimpse the distance which separates the nice from the good, and the vision of this gap had terrified his soul. He had seen, far off, what is perhaps the most dreadful thing in the world, the other face of love, its blank face. Everything that he was, even the best that he was, was connected with possessive self-filling human love. That blank demand implied the death of his whole being. The old man [in the monastery] was right to say that one should start young. Perhaps it was to calm the frenzy of this fear that he had so much and so suddenly needed to hold tightly in his arms a beautiful golden-skinned boy as lithe as a puma. What happened afterwards was hideous graceless confusion, the familiar deceitful jumble of himself breaking forth again in a scene from which he thought it had disappeared forever.

Theo's problem thus resembles that of Michael in *The Bell* whose Christian priestly vocation foundered for the same reason.

In this renunciation of the desiring self, there is a hint of Buddhist and Hindu values, just as in Willy Kost's speech to Jessica, he insists that there is a lower-case grace that will aid one in attaining virtue, and thus echoes a central concept of Christianity. As is usual with Miss Murdoch, these fundamentally religious ideas are presented in a secular context for secular application.

As has been emphasized several times before, the major moral accommodations of this novel are those of persons who must come to terms with their past, learn to live with the fruits of past actions, and where the past is redeemable, the attempt is made, as when Paula and Richard attempt a reconciliation, and when Theo considers returning to the Indian monastery to live out his remaining years.

We have noted that despite her general attainment of openness in this novel, Miss Murdoch fairly frequently (and helplessly) falls back into neat patternings; this is no more evident, in relation to the theme of returning to the past, than in Chapter 17. All three of the Trescombe ladies (whom we accompanied in Chapter 14 on a walk on the beach, each absorbed in a parallel *monologue intérieur*) go to London, each on a trumped-up errand: Kate Gray goes to John Ducane's home to see his chauffeur; Mary Clothier walks by her former home where her husband died; Paula Biranne walks by her former home, only to see an elegantly clad lady entering her husband's door; and, for good measure, John's mistress Jessica (whom he is trying to make a thing of the past) walks by his home just in time to see Kate Gray going in the door. Discounting Kate, who is preternaturally happy in her ignorance and ignorantly happy, we have concentrated here the problems of women with pasts: the widow, the divorcée, and the abandoned mistress, all haunting places associated with a once-live love.

Mary Clothier lost her husband in a scene, reenacted in her mind as she passes the old home, that closely resembles (perhaps by accident) a famous scene in Nabokov's *Lolita*. Alistair went out to mail a letter, still hot from a marital squabble, and was accidentally run down by an automobile before Mary's horrified eyes. She is trying, by reliving this scene, to master the guilt and the unresolved recriminations of that period in her life, in order to give herself more completely to Willy Kost, with whom she is momentarily in love.

Much later in the novel, after having been rejected twice by Willy, Mary sits in a boat outside the grotto where John has swum in to find her son Pierce; she experiences a moving meditation on what it means to love the dead, with the haunting fear that her son may already have drowned:

> Death happens, love happens, and all human life is compact of
> accident and chance. If one loves what is so frail and mortal, if

one loves and holds on, like a terrier holding on, must not one's love become changed? There is only one absolute imperative, the imperative to love: yet how can one endure to go on loving what must die, what indeed is dead? . . . One is oneself this piece of earth, this concoction of frailty, a momentary shadow upon the chaos of the accidental world. Since death and chance are the material of all there is, if love is to be love of something it must be love of death and chance. This changed love moves upon the ocean of accident, over the forms of the dead, a love so impersonal and so cold it can scarcely be recognized, a love devoid of beauty, of which one knows no more than the name, so little is it like an experience.

Immediately following this meditation her son Pierce, who was bent on suicide, and John Ducane, the man she will ultimately marry, appear in the water, revenants from a very close brush with death.

Paula, the divorcée, is caught up on a past experience even more traumatic than Mary's sight of her husband's accident, because she is more culpable. Although Richard had been a particularly unfaithful husband, Paula had betrayed him only once, with Eric, a nasty, weak, parasitic person; Richard, as is perhaps typical of persons who are unfaithful themselves, proves insanely jealous, and when he discovers the lovers together, up-ends a heavy billiard table on Eric's foot, necessitating its amputation. Now, years later, Paula is in anguish due to a series of letters from the demonic Eric, who says he is returning from Australia and from her past to claim her as his eternal woman. Just when John is doing his best to advise Paula on how to handle Eric during this confrontation, a letter arrives saying he met an American heiress on the ship, who is his current eternal woman. Released from this bond with the past, though, Paula is forced, by the terms of John's private justice with Richard in the Radeechy suicide case, to attempt a reconciliation with her former husband, and to live with the knowledge of his former insane violence.

In a somewhat Proustian touch, we learn that Richard's love for Paula centers about a Bronzino canvas in the National Gallery, "Venus, Cupid, Folly, and Time." And it is before this work that Richard insists he and Paula make their first new contact. In a scene of virtuoso writing that is dazzling in its beauty, complexity, humor, and intelligence, Miss Murdoch presents a love scene between two mature and shopworn middle-aged persons that incorporates a perspicacious but lyrical form of art criticism. Aside from Proust's passages on the Botticelli frescoes in the Sistine Chapel, and perhaps one or two Huxley scenes in this area, it is unequalled in modern literature for its sophistication, wit, and dry intelligence. As their desire for each other mounts inexorably throughout the scene, their troubled parrying for terms on which to come together is paralleled by allegorical readings from the canvas; Richard cannot promise complete fidelity, Paula is not yet sure she can suppress the memory of his violence, he finds it difficult to confess his complicity in the Radeechy case—and over all of this brood Love, Time, Deceit, Jealousy, Pleasure, Cupid, and Venus. By the time of their ultimate agreement, they seem to dash from the room to avoid disgraceful public fornication, Richard running back to brush his fingers over the luscious lips of Venus and Cupid. The scene is a capstone to earlier attempts at similar effects, notably Bledyard's art lecture in *The Sandcastle*, Dora Greenfield's ecstatic vision before a canvas in the same gallery, in *The Bell*, and the handling of the Tintoretto in *An Unofficial Rose*.

Jessica Bird, the abandoned mistress, is perhaps not so important in herself as the other women, serving more as one of the poles of John's confused moral dilemma (he is stringing her along at the same time he is flirting with Kate Gray, unable to tell either one about the other). She is a direct descendant, in Miss Murdoch's artistic family, of Dora Greenfield (*The Bell*) in her character, and of Georgie Hands (*A Severed Head*) in her life situation. Like Dora (and, incidentally rather resembling Pattie O'Driscoll of *The Time of the Angels*), she is barren of all conceptualization or mental generalizations, the pagan art-student drifter almost totally without moral sense, accustomed to copulation with her "strict contemporaries" in the presence of others because space is limited and no one cares anyway. She soon comes to cling to the forty-three-year-old John Ducane because he seems to embody a stability and authority totally lacking in her contemporaries; but like Paul Greenfield, John completely fails to teach Jessica the art history she so desperately needs in order even to understand herself as a student and as a teacher. The gulf between them, which constituted the primary appeal in the first place, remains a yawning chasm of non-communication. But when John attempts to fight free, Jessica browbeats and intimidates him by brute tears, hysteria, and panic. She comes closest to being an elemental, blind emotional force.

Her parallel to Mary's and Paula's visits to their former homes is two-fold. In passing John's home, as we have seen, she observes Kate Gray entering; later she steals into his home at a time when Willy Kost is a houseguest, representing herself as a decorator, and searches his bedroom for telltale marks of "the other woman." It is one of those piquant scenes where Miss Murdoch is at her best in combining a rich catalogue of objects and clothes with tense suspense; and then the sudden surprise of Willy's entry and exposure of her disguise, which leads to his taking her immediately on the bed. It is during this encounter that Willy lectures Jessica on the basic immorality of her kind of frenzied jealousy, ultimately reproving her because she wants to be dependent on others without really desiring to be helped by them. Although acting as if she were possessed by a demon, she pursues John as if she were a demonic force herself.

Willy, despite all the impressive moral authority of his pronouncements, has in at least one instance lied to Mary in maintaining he is impotent; but he is apparently honest in saying he cannot sustain any relationships with others; he tells Jessica, as he takes her on John's bed, that they must consider this incident an "island of joy" with no before or after. But for the clinging Jessica, such islands are inconceivable; true to form, she pursues him to the country where Theo, in a fiendish trick, perfectly negates Willy's carefully wrought plans to escape the confrontation. Finally, in a novel notable for the slickness with which loose fibers are woven into the denouement—when even the scrapping cat and dog share the same basket—Jessica remains one of the imponderable ciphers.

Thus these women carry the burden of the theme dealing with accommodations to moral messes from the past, on a human plane of love (the nice) where they learn the lesson Miss Murdoch repeatedly reiterates, that of cherishing the real otherness of real other persons; Theo contributes a major harmony, since the revelation of his experience at the monastery is the last major unveiling in the novel, and in the meditation already quoted, he enunciates the possibility of a selfless spiritual love (the good).

The focus for much of the thematic content, however, is John Ducane, partially because he is the avuncular ear for all the disturbed characters, who attribute to him powers as a dispenser of advice and consolation rather beyond anything the reader can observe for himself in John's character. John's own agonized moral progress has many stages, which can only be sketched out here.

On the one hand, as investigator of the Radeechy suicide, he must make the choice of revealing or withholding information about Claudia Radeechy's murder (her husband pushed her out a window during an acrimonious argument about her affair with Richard Biranne, and since Richard witnessed it all, he is technically an accessory). In addition, Richard used this information to try to steal Judy McGrath from Radeechy. We have seen that in this case, John decided on private "justice" on his own condition—once he is convinced that Richard has suffered sufficient remorse—of a reconciliation with Paula in which Richard confesses his part in the Radeechy affair. This decision was based in part on John's knowledge of his own moral shortcomings: he has kept both Jessica and Kate on the string simultaneously, although he already meant to break with Jessica, and Kate never meant for their affair to reach the stage of physical manifestation. In addition, he has heavily suppressed homosexual inclinations toward his chauffeur and toward Peter McGrath, the office messenger, who had been blackmailing Radeechy, failed in his attempt to blackmail Biranne, but has mild success for a while in blackmailing John about Jessica and Kate.

Thirdly, John is enormously drawn toward McGrath's wife Judy, a statuesque, magnetic, maddeningly desirable golden beauty, the "Helen of Troy" of the whole scandal, who specializes in enslaving highly placed functionaries with peculiar sexual tastes, and then blackmailing them through her husband's prowess with a camera. Especially in John's resistance to the determined Judy—who repeatedly shows up stark naked in lusciously appealing slants of light as John casually opens doors—does he begin to put a little moral starch into his hitherto lax moral behavior.

But it is his terrifyingly close acquaintance with death, when he swims into the grotto to rescue Pierce, that convinces him, in a passage quoted earlier, that forgiveness and reconciliation are all that matter. It is John who is also the prime mover in uniting the various couples: he reconciles Paula and Richard; he strikes Pierce for torturing Barbara by sequestering her cat, and thus tries to teach Pierce the patience that is all he can practice in the face of Barbara's coldness; and he attempts to unite Mary Clothier with Willy Kost before he finally marries her himself. At the servant level, he pairs Judy McGrath and Fivey, his chauffeur, by asking the latter to drive Judy home after one of her temptress acts in his bedroom.

I have already suggested that "the nice" and "the good" of the title refer, respectively, to the kind of human love represented by the many pairings-off in the final chapters and to a selfless, transcendent spiritual love. A kind of selflessness, however, is common to the best of both loves. John sees the far-reaching destructiveness that results from the lack of this kind of love, as he contemplates the presumptuous acrostic he had copied from the wall of the chambers where Radeechy conducted black masses:

> Ducane could not see into that world [of the occult]. He saw only the grotesque and the childish, and whatever was frightening here seemed to be something of limited power, something small. . . . The great evil, the dreadful evil, that which made war and slavery and all man's inhumanity to man lay in the cool self-justifying ruthless selfishness of quite ordinary people, such as Biranne, and himself.

Thus the course of the novel is toward exorcism of the obsessive demons

of selfish preoccupation, usually with past events. Paula overcomes her traumatic obsession with Richard's violence toward Eric, just as Richard cleanses
his past by confession to her; Mary resolves her guilt for Alistair's accidental
death; John releases himself from the deadlock of Jessica's possessiveness and
Kate's playful kitten love.

There is, then, a fairly insistent imaging of demonic possession in this
novel. In the past, Miss Murdoch frequently resorted to a metaphorical
demonology in her characterization, especially in treating the recurrent East
European refugee type—a device reminiscent of Muriel Spark's treatment of
the protagonist of *The Ballad of Peckham Rye*. With *The Time of the Angels*,
this same imagery gained a kind of theoretical justification in the doctrines
of Father Carel, the "God is dead" theologian, who sees such demons as
wandering, detached ideas split off from a concept of God which was once
unitary, but in our fragmented age, His Ideas become destructive, malignant
angels. The idea recurs in this novel, but with a completely secular emphasis:

> There are mysterious agencies of the human mind which, like
> roving gases, travel the world, causing pain and mutilation,
> without their owners' having any full awareness, or even any
> awareness at all, of the strength and the whereabouts of these
> exhalations. Possibly a saint might be known by the utter absence
> of such gaseous tentacles, but the ordinary person is naturally
> endowed with them, just as he is endowed with the ghostly power
> of appearing in other people's dreams. So it is that we can be
> terrors to each other, and people in lonely rooms suffer humili-
> ation and even damage because of others in whose consciousness
> perhaps they scarcely figure at all. Eidola projected from the mind
> take on a life of their own, wandering to find their victims and
> maddening them with miseries and fears which the original source
> of these wanderers could not be justly charged with inflicting
> and might indeed be puzzled to hear of.

But whatever the source of the demons, love is the exorciser. As John learns
when he and Mary come to their miraculous mutual understanding, "No
love is entirely without worth, even when the frivolous calls to the frivolous
and the base to the base. But it is in the nature of love to discern good,
and the best love is in some part at any rate a love of what is good."

LOUIS L. MARTZ

The London Novels

London in the summer of 1970 is filled with the presence of Charles
Dickens. His benevolent, bearded countenance glides by on the Underground
escalators; he is advertising his superb Centennial Exhibition (at the Victoria
and Albert), which includes everything from his cuff links to the manuscript
of *Bleak House*. Meanwhile, London Transport is advertising its excellent
paperback: *The London of Charles Dickens*, an index of one hundred sixty pages
describing virtually all the London sites and streets mentioned in Dickens'
writings, with nostalgic, evocative quotations and careful accounts of the
action that occurred in each place. Thus under "Foster Lane" there is first
a quotation from *Martin Chuzzlewit*: "A dim, dirty, smoky, tumble-down,
rotten old house it was as anybody would desire to see." And then follows
the explanation: "No. 5 Foster Lane (Priest's Court) is pointed out as very
likely premises for the Chuzzlewits, father and son, having a side entrance
which was found so useful by Jonas when planning the alibi for his murder
of Montague Tigg." Under "St. Magnus's Church" we read: "On the night
that Nancy had a secret meeting with Rose Maylie and Mr. Brownlow on
London Bridge steps, Dickens describes the murky night while the girl, and
the sinister figure following her, were still. 'The tower of old Saint Saviour's
Church, and the spire of Saint Magnus, so long the giant-warders of the
ancient bridge, were visible in the gloom; but the forest of shipping below
bridge, and the thickly scattered spires of churches above, were nearly all
hidden from sight.' *Oliver Twist* Ch. XLVI." Under "Grosvenor Square"
there is a startling contrast with the present-day scene: "Mr. Tite Barnacle

From *Twentieth-Century Literature in Retrospect*. © 1971 by the President and Fellows of Harvard
College. Harvard University Press, 1971. Originally entitled "Iris Murdoch: The London
Novels."

resided here at No. 24, Mews Street, Grosvenor Square, 'a hideous little street of dead walls, stables, and dunghills, with lofts over coach-houses inhabited by coachmen's families, who had a passion for drying clothes, and decorating their window-sills with miniature turnpike-gates . . .' *Little Dorrit* Book i, Ch. X." To choose just one more example, under "Bryanston Square" we find simply this long quotation from *Dombey and Son*:

> Mr. Dombey's house was a large one, on the shady side of a tall, dark, dreadfully genteel street in the region between Portland Place and Bryanston Square. It was a corner house, with great wide areas containing cellars frowned upon by barred windows, and leered at by crooked-eyed doors leading to dustbins. It was a house of dismal state, with a circular back to it, containing a whole suite of drawing-rooms looking upon a gravelled yard, where two gaunt trees, with blackened trunks and branches rattled rather than rustled, their leaves were so smoke dried.

In this atmosphere of the Centennial Year, it seems appropriate to celebrate also the achievement of the living writer who is, in her London novels, the most important heir to the Dickens tradition. One would not have said this two or three years ago because the Dickensian use of London scenes that marked Iris Murdoch's first novel, *Under the Net* (1954), was not a dominant characteristic in any of the nine novels that so quickly followed; it is only in her last three, and especially the last two, *Bruno's Dream* (1969) and *A Fairly Honourable Defeat* (1970), that the Dickensian vein in her use of London scenes has strongly reemerged. If Miss Murdoch continues to write in this vein (as I hope she will) it may not be pure fantasy to imagine an exhibition or an index containing entries such as these:

> Boltons, The. S.W. 10. An elegant oval, well shrubbed, with Saint Mary The Boltons in the center, which stands as a green and white oasis in the region between the Old Brompton Road and the Fulham Road. In *A Fairly Honourable Defeat* (Ch. VIII), Morgan frantically pursues Julius along "the left hand curve" of the oval toward the Brompton Road, while Julius, invisible to her, is walking along the right hand curve. They meet at the north end, to Julius' irritation.

> Brompton Cemetery. S.W. 10. Located between the Old Brompton Road and the Fulham Road. "Big houselike tombs, the dwellings of the dead, lined the wide central walk which

showed in a cold sunny glimpse the curve of distant pillars. In quieter side avenues humbler graves were straggled about with grass, with here and there a cleared place, a chained space, a clipped mound, a body's length of granite chips, a few recent flowers wilting beside a name. Above the line of mist-green budding lime trees there rose far off the three black towers of Lots Road power station" *Bruno's Dream* (Ch. XVI). Danby waits feverishly behind the iron fence at the Brompton Road end for Lisa to walk by on her way home to Miles's house in Kempsford Gardens (see below).

Hammersmith Mall. W. 6. Accurately described in *Under the Net* (Ch. III): "a labyrinth of waterworks and laundries with pubs and Georgian houses in between, which sometimes face the river and sometimes back it." Jake, searching for Anna, goes to a certain address here "on that part of the Mall that lies between the Doves and the Black Lion." These two pubs mark the eastern and the western extremities of Upper Mall. "The number to which I had been directed turned out to be a house standing a little by itself, with its back to the river and its front on a quiet piece of street, and an opening beside it where some steps led down to the water . . . It was a brooding self-absorbed sort of house, fronted by a small ragged garden and a wall shoulder high. The house was square, with rows of tall windows, and had preserved a remnant of elegance." At the east end of that part of Upper Mall accessible to motor cars, the house numbered 21 (next to the Doves) answers this description quite well except for the squareness and the tall windows; these details seem to be adapted from William Morris' Kelmscott House, which faces the river a few yards away. The stairs down to the river are in front of Kelmscott House.

Holborn Viaduct. E.C. 1. The bridge over Farringdon Street from which Jake and his companions start their pub tour in search of Hugo: "We stood beside the iron lions on the Viaduct. The intense light of evening fell upon the spires and towers of St. Bride to the south, St. James to the north, St. Andrew to the west, and St. Sepulchre, and St. Leonard Foster and St. Mary-le-Bow to the east. The evening light quieted the houses and the abandoned white spires. Farringdon Street was still wide and

empty," *Under the Net* (Ch. VII). The view is now (1971) eclipsed
by new construction. From beside the lions at the four corners
of the Viaduct one can see at most only two towers, Bow Church
and Christ Church (which the novel calls St. Leonard Foster—a
church destroyed in the Great Fire and never rebuilt).

Lots Road. S.W. 10. In *Bruno's Dream* the site of the power
station whose chimneys loom (protectively or menacingly?) over
Danby's house on Stadium Street. There are only two chimneys;
the novel's "trinity of towers" (Ch. IV) is perhaps a symbolic
touch.

And so on, page after page. The kinship with Dickens is, I hope,
evident from all the above citations; but more important than any particular
scene is the underlying kinship in basic function. Both Dickens and Miss
Murdoch need this particularity of detail because they present so many of
these London characters as inseparable from the London setting. Houses,
streets, and squares become part of the personalities living in each particular
location. "Like all true Earls Courters, Ducane despised Chelsea. The bounder
[Biranne] would live in a place like this, he said to himself, as he turned
into Smith Street and began to pass along the line of smartly painted hall
doors." Thus in Dickens Mrs. Todgers is inseparable from her boarding
house under the shadow of the Monument; in Murdoch, Bruno and his
beloved spiders are inseparable from the damp, decrepit room in which he
is breathing so tenaciously his last days.

The London novels of Iris Murdoch have their Dickensian quality of
detail because they grow from a deep, instinctive affection for the London
setting, whether sordid, shabby, or genteel. And that affection for the
outward traces of man's habitation derives from the theme of love that
constitutes the redemptive element in the novels of both writers. Danby
loves that shabby house in its decaying place:

He loved the little yard outside his window, below ground level,
always dark and covered in slippery green moss. It was always
called "the yard," never "the garden" although it had a yellow
privet bush and a laurel bush and a rose that had reverted to
briar. The soil was black and no grass would grow on it, only a
few dandelions and weedy marigolds which struggled up each
year through the damp crust of the moss. The chimneys of Lots
Road power station towered above, suitable extensions of that
murky infertile earth.

Somehow Danby's love is inseparable from this earthy atmosphere. Likewise, Danby loves his job at the printing plant: "He loved the works, the clattering noise, the papery dust, the tribal independence of the printers, he loved the basic stuff of the trade, the clean-cut virginal paper, the virile elemental lead." And we learn that "he was fond of the machines, especially the older simpler ones"; he collects with love old printing presses. He loves women too, a good many of them, in various ways; but best of all is his great love for his dead wife, Bruno's "intense and high and spiritual" daughter—who herself died of love in a way, for she jumped off Battersea Bridge and drowned in an effort to save a child who had fallen in the river. This quality of deep, spontaneous affection in Danby accounts for the way in which he proves attractive to the most unlikely women.

Miles, Bruno's son, despises Danby and cannot understand why his own sister (and later the similar character Lisa) could possibly have fallen in love with so ordinary, unintellectual a person. But Miles is severely limited in the range of his own affections. He is so obsessively attached to the memory of his dead Indian bride, Parvati, that he really cannnot apprehend any other human being. Even his second wife Diana seems neglected and has to seek an outlet for her affections in the furnishings of the small house in Kempsford Gardens.

Bruno, above all, is limited in love. He failed his wife first through infidelity and then he failed her at her death, forty years before the novel opens; he ignored her death-bed cries, fearing that she would damn him if he answered. And Bruno failed his son by not attempting to understand the marriage with Parvati; he has been utterly cut off from Miles for many years. And yet, enclosed now in this one moldy room in his last long illness, Bruno is not wholly cut off from affection. He loves spiders; he speaks their names as if they were human; to him they are beings worthy of love. His unwritten books on spiders are his "Books of Particulars," akin to the "Notebook of Particulars" by which Miles strives to keep his affections alive while he waits for the Muse to come. And at the very end of *Bruno's Dream* we note, by Diana's new grasp of particulars, the signs that she is rescued from her barren existence by her affectionate care for Bruno:

> As she sat day after day holding Bruno's gaunt blotched hand in her own she puzzled over the pain and what it was and where it was, whether in her or in Bruno. And she saw the ivy leaves and the puckered door knob, and the tear in the pocket of Bruno's old dressing gown with a clarity and a closeness which she had never experienced before. The familiar roads between Kempsford

> Gardens and Stadium Street seemed like those of an unknown
> city, so many were the new things which she now began to notice
> in them: potted plants in windows, irregular stains upon walls,
> moist green moss between paving stones. Even little piles of dust
> and screwed up paper drifted into corners seemed to claim and
> deserve her attention. And the faces of passersby glowed with
> uncanny clarity, as if her specious present had been lengthened
> out to allow of contemplation within the space of a second. Diana
> wondered what it meant.

What it means is that Diana has been redeemed through love, in Danby's
house, in Bruno's room, in Bruno's dream. This scene is one that draws
together the whole fine novel into an effective unity. The streets, the characters, the particulars of place and scene—all grow together, strands of the
consciousness that extends from the dying mind of Bruno. All events of the
novel have in one way or another been "caused by some emanation from
that awful room in Stadium Street."

So, in her twelfth and best novel Miss Murdoch has returned, with
greatly enriched powers, to the action of a central consciousness within a
London setting and also to the basic, unobtrusive themes of her first novel,
Under the Net. But one cannot, I think, find the essential relation between
these two books by dealing with them as "philosophical novels" and by
using, as is sometimes done, frequent references to Sartre, Kant, Simone
Weil, Hegel, or Wittgenstein (although interpretations of this kind are
valuable in illuminating some of the latent concepts within the novels). It
is true that Miss Murdoch's first book was a monograph on Sartre (published
in 1953, one year before *Under the Net*), and that it throws a great deal of
light on her first novel. Moreover, she has given some validity to the relationship between this novel and the thought of Wittgenstein because she
has herself said that the title refers to Wittgenstein's "net" of concepts and
theories. And it is true that Jake, the protagonist and narrator of *Under the
Net*, thinks of himself as a sort of rootless, solipsistic character out of some
modern French novel; but the reasons for this are not far to seek. On the
opening page of the book Jake is returning from Paris with his suitcases
"full of French books and very heavy"; he makes a little money by translating
a current French novelist ("Breteuil"), but he is astonished and dismayed
when he learns that this novelist has won the Prix Goncourt. The point, I
think, is this: Jake has his head and his suitcases full of undigested modern
thought, especially French existential thought, but he does not really grasp
its meaning. His real self exists elsewhere, and his problem is to find it.

The clue to that essential self lies also on this novel's opening page, in his statement "until I have been able to bury my head so deep in dear London that I can forget that I have ever been away I am inconsolable." Jake's deep affection for and acute consciousness of particular places in the London scene serve ironically to show how securely rooted he really is in his "beloved city," of which he knows every detail from Cannon Street to the Goldhawk Road.

Since this is a novel told in the first person, the response to detail, the memory of places, forms an essential part of the character whose mind is here being created. Jake pursues a dream of love for Anna; he misunderstands *all* the human characters about him; but he is nevertheless rooted and he will be saved, because he is capable of perceiving at last the truth about himself. When at the end, in desperation, he decides to take a job as hospital orderly, he says he is amazed and impressed by the fact that he can do the job so well. But we the readers should not be surprised, for he has shown in all his responses to the London scene a firm grip on detail and a resourceful, unfailing ability to move from spot to spot in search of a goal. The comical pub tour [in the novel] is an indication of his basic grip on external things: "We strode past St. Sepulchre and straight into the Viaduct Tavern, which is a Meux's house . . . There was a sleek Charrington's house called the Magpie and Stump . . . The George is an agreeable Watney's house with peeling walls and an ancient counter with one of those cut-glass and mahogany superstructures." And so on from pub to pub, most of them still standing, though in greatly changed surroundings.

In the process of this tour Iris Murdoch creates the vision of a vanished scene. It is in fact almost as hard to trace this tour of "Iris Murdoch's London" as it is to trace Dickens' London, since the bombed-out City in which this tour occurs has now been so thoroughly rebuilt. That is why such a passage as this has about it the nostalgic quality so often found in Dickens' descriptions:

> From the darkness and shade of St. Paul's Churchyard we came into Cheapside as into a bright arena, and saw framed in the gap of a ruin the pale neat rectangles of St. Nicholas Cole Abbey, standing alone away to the south of us on the other side of Cannon Street. In between the willow herb waved over what remained of streets. In this desolation the coloured shells of houses still raised up filled and blank squares of wall and window. The declining sun struck on glowing bricks and flashing tiles and warmed the stone of an occasional fallen pillar. As we passed St.

top of the sky was vibrating into a later blue, and turning into
what used to be Freeman's Court we entered a Henekey's house.

(Under the Net)

Finally, as they make their way down toward a redeeming swim in the
Thames, we have a scene that seems even closer to the quality of Dickens:

> Across a moonswept open space we followed what used to be
> Fyefoot Lane, where many a melancholy notice board tells in the
> ruins of the City where churches and where public houses once
> stood. Beside the solitary tower of St. Nicholas we passed into
> Upper Thames Street. There was no sound; not a bell, not a
> footstep. We trod softly. We turned out of the moonlight into
> a dark labyrinth of alleys and gutted warehouses where indistin-
> guishable objects loomed in piles. Scraps of newspaper blotted
> the streets, immobilized in the motionless night. The rare street
> lamps revealed pitted brick walls and cast the shadow of an
> occasional cat. A street as deep and dark as a well ended at last
> in a stone breakwater, and on the other side, at the foot of a few
> steps, was the moon again, scattered in pieces upon the river.
> We climbed over on to the steps and stood in silence for a while
> with the water lapping our feet.

By comparison, after all these London details, Jake's subsequent trip
to Paris turns out to be a journey into illusion. As he says: "Arriving in
Paris always causes me pain, even when I have been away for only a short
while. It is a city which I never fail to approach with expectation and leave
with disappointment . . . Paris remains for me still an unresolved harmony.
It is the only city which I can personify." Yes, he can personify Paris, make
the city into a kind of remote goddess; but he cannot do this for London,
which, as he says, "I know too well." And so the whole long account of
Paris, in spite of its frequent detail, takes on the atmosphere of a dream or
nightmare, an effect epitomized in the closing scene, where he pursues what
he thinks is the figure of Anna into the darkness of the Tuileries Gardens.
He "loses" her, but it seems likely that she was never there, for the woman
he finally calls to turns out not to be Anna. This account of Paris is filled
with sentimental, overwrought views: "If like myself you are a connoisseur
of solitude, I recommend to you the experience of being alone in Paris on
the fourteenth of July. On that day the city lets down its tumultuous hair,
which the high summer anoints with warmth and perfume. In Paris every
man has his girl; but on that day every man is a sultan. Then people flock

together and sweep chattering about the city like flights of brilliantly coloured birds." One might add, "Unreal City."

How absurd it is for such a devoted pub crawler to dramatize himself as "a connoisseur of solitude"! In fact, he hates solitude; the novel consists of his continual search for companionship, with Anna, with Hugo, with the dog Mars. And he greatly enjoys being with the nurses and patients at the hospital:

> I would sit under one of the trees, while Mars bounded about close by, giving his attention now to one tree and now to another, and the young nurses of Corelli would come and gather round me like nymphs and laugh at me and say that I looked like a wise man sitting cross-legged under my tree, and admire Mars and make much of him, and defend me against Stitch, who would have liked to have forbidden me to have Mars in the garden at all. I enjoyed these lunch times.
>
> It was in the afternoon that I managed at last to see something of the patients. But this wasn't until the later afternoon. I looked forward to this all day. In my apprehension of it, the Hospital declined through a scale of decreasing degrees of reality in proportion to the distance away from the patients. They were the centre to which all else was peripheral.

And when he can think of no one else to seek out, he finds solace in the enigmatic presence of the Soho shopkeeper Mrs. Tinckham and her cats. Jake loves people, pets, and places: he is as different from Camus's Stranger or Sartre's Roquentin as it is possible for a man to be.

Return to London brings the hospital job, along with the realization of the various truths about Hugo and Anna and Sadie and Finn. The final taxi ride from Kensington to the Holborn Viaduct marks a return to the source, telling the tale of a man who has never quite been lost and whose individual will has been restored:

> I left the pub. I was somewhere in the Fulham Road. I waited quietly upon the kerb until I saw a taxi approaching. I hailed it. "Holborn Viaduct," I said to the driver. I lay back in the taxi; and as I did so I felt that this was the last action for a very long time that would seem to me to be inevitable. London sped past me, beloved city, almost invisible in its familiarity. South Kensington, Knightsbridge, Hyde Park Corner. This was the last act which would provoke no question and require no reason.

> After this would come the long agony of reflection. London passed
> before me like the life of a drowning man which they say flashes
> upon him all at once in the final moment. Piccadilly, Shaftesbury
> Avenue, New Oxford Street, High Holborn.

The "dark London boyhood" which Jake mentions early in the novel has
become, like Dickens' own boyhood, the sign and the source of his renewal.

What happened in Miss Murdoch's next nine novels, gradually moving
away from, weaving in and out of, and finally returning to London, is a
story of intense experimentation with many different modes. After this
beginning with Dickens-cum-Sartre, she seems to have been impelled toward
an extended exploration of the many techniques available to the modern
practitioner of fiction. It is a remarkable story, worth sketching briefly in
order to show the varying roles that London has played in her career.

Miss Murdoch's second novel, *The Flight from the Enchanter* (1956), also
occurs in London except for the fade-out in France and on the shores of Italy,
where Rosa forsakes, through fear, the unhappy exile Mischa Fox, whom
she might have saved from his empty pursuit of power and his hopeless
effort to recover the memory of a lost European childhood. But the novel
is only located, it is not really set, in London; the lack of detail is surprising
in comparison with *Under the Net*: "Rosa ran down the road towards the
factory. The big square building with its square windows grew larger and
larger until it was looming over her. A tall chimney held a motionless trail
of white smoke over three streets and the width of the Thames." "They
walked the length of two streets and then turned into a rather dark mews,
where it seemed to have been raining." "Mischa had had the fantasy of
buying four houses in Kensington, two adjoining in one road, and two
adjoining in the next road, and standing back to back with the first two."
But what roads, what streets? One would never ask the question in *Under
the Net* or *Bruno's Dream*.

Only the setting of Rainborough's house and garden is given anything
like the detail of these other novels, and for good reason. "His home was a
safe stronghold; it had been the home of his childhood, and it was full of
myths and spirits from the past, whose beneficent murmur could be heard
as soon as he had stilled his mind and put away the irritations of his day at
the office." As he stands in his garden he discovers his own Book of
Particulars:

> Hyacinths, narcissi, primulas, and daffodils stood before him,
> rigid with life and crested with stamens, tight in circles, or
> expanding into stars. He looked down into their black and golden

hearts; and as he looked the flower-bed seemed to become very large and close and detailed. He began to see the little hairs upon the stems of the flowers and the yellow grains of pollen, and where a small snail, still almost transparent with extreme youth, was slowly putting out its horns upon a leaf. Near to his foot an army of ants had made a two-way track across the path. He watched the ants. Each one knows what it is doing, he thought. He looked at the snail. Can it see me? he wondered. Then he felt, how little I know, and how little it is possible to know; and with this thought he experienced a moment of joy.

Here and only here Rainborough enjoys a clarification of vision. He is rooted in this old home, but he is being uprooted, first by the encroachment of the hospital extension and second by the aggressions of the intrepid Miss Casement. Fleeing from her clutches and her red MG, he is provided with a refuge in France by the cosmopolitan Marcia.

Rosa, who might have saved some of these exiles, saves no one, not even herself. Rosa represents the kind of welfare worker whose only welfare lies in her own self-satisfaction. Having "saved" the two Polish refugees, the beautiful Lusiewicz brothers, she becomes their willing victim in lust. And the brothers turn out to be vile: cruel to the world that has been cruel to them. Appropriately in this novel of rootless beings, the Dickensian details of a truly London setting do not emerge. The book could as well, or perhaps better, have been set in Los Angeles or Chicago. Yet even here one feels a few traces of Dickens—in the character of that splendid eccentric Mrs. Wingfield, ancient defender of women's rights. The account of her house and person, the scene of the meeting of the board of *Artemis* (ancient magazine of women's liberation)—these are skillful Dickensian touches. But the novel, for all its brilliance, is not as satisfying as *Under the Net*. It lacks the cohesion of a firm setting within a central consciousness and within this "beloved city."

Miss Murdoch's third novel, *The Sandcastle* (1957), has been called by someone a novel best read under the hairdryer. Exactly: it is quite deliberately, I think, designed in the popular mode of fiction for the woman's magazine. Here is the middle-aged couple stuck in their suburban house in Surrey, not a long run from Waterloo Station, with two growing children and a growing boredom in each other's presence. Then in comes a lovely young thing, in the person of a portrait-painter; soon the hero is reluctantly swept away by a strange passion, while Nan, the wife, has to fight for her marriage and wins by bold ingenious action. Trite? Of course, but what

Miss Murdoch makes of these conventional materials is unusual, for the chief characters (and some of the minor figures, such as the stammering art teacher, Bledyard) develop into persons of depth and poignancy far beyond the range of the chosen literary model. It is as though the author, somewhat dismayed by the way in which the teeming characters of *Flight from the Enchanter* had refused to cohere, had decided to discipline her powers by working with a small cast within a strictly conventional plot.

The Bell (1958), Miss Murdoch's fourth novel, ranges out again into a large cast. The few London scenes offer a counterpoint to the main setting, an Anglican retreat next to a nunnery in Gloucestershire. This highly successful novel seems to derive from a blending of two models: George Eliot and D. H. Lawrence, especially the latter. One feels the presence of Lawrence in certain efforts at lyrical description of nature, but one feels it more strongly in the two chief characters. Dora, fleeing from her harsh, demanding, intellectual husband, manages to mature and win freedom in this country scene. Her act of ringing the great bell signals her liberation from the arid forces that would deny her nature. Michael, struggling to subdue his homosexual tendency, reminds one a little of Lawrence's Gerald: an earnest, tormented, and ultimately lost man. This novel deals with a basic Lawrencian theme: the anguish and death caused by failures "to touch."

The three-year lapse before the appearance of Miss Murdoch's fifth novel, *A Severed Head* (1961), perhaps represents a time of severe reappraisal in her career. This is the period of her Yale lectures, devoted to the theory of the novel and affirming her loyalty to the nineteenth-century novel of character. It is all the more surprising, then, that *A Severed Head* should bear so little resemblance to the novelists praised in these lectures: Scott, Jane Austen, George Eliot, Tolstoy. The peculiar mode of the book emerges clearly from its dramatization by Miss Murdoch and J. B. Priestley. The revolving stage, with its shifting of bedrooms, drawing rooms, and partners, reveals the basic mode of Restoration comedy, the comedy of manners—along with a good many touches of Dickensian caricature. Though it is located for the most part in London, the only significant London quality is the symbolic (Dickensian) fog representing the muddle in the mind of the narrator, Martin Lynch-Gibbon. The characters are equally Philadelphian or Bostonian; and indeed, the rootless psychiatrist, Palmer Anderson, is an American of sorts, though we learn that his mother was Scottish, that he was brought up in Europe, and that he has lived some years in Japan. Out of the fog emerges (at Liverpool Station) the rugged, earthy, rather ferocious figure of Honor Klein, whose role has sometimes been found incongruous. But incongruity is her function. With her flashing samurai ritual, her incestuous relations with her half-brother, and here tough, direct speech, she cuts out cant, she shocks with truth, she reveals all and is ashamed of nothing. No wonder the sophistications of this modern Restoration comedy wither away under the onslaught of her formidable powers.

The sixth novel, *An Unofficial Rose* (1962), shifts its primary setting to a country house, with secondary scenes in a London flat. But London is not really a presence here. The real presence is Henry James: the style is in places deliberately Jamesian with, at times, something close to pointed parody. These touches are simply ways of signalling the mode, and we can and should go on to apprehend the brilliance of the way in which the author handles the delicate, slowly developing perceptions.

The Unicorn (1963) presents a violent contrast to the intricate nuances and slow discriminations of the Jamesian novel. Miss Murdoch here turns to create a Gothic novel based on the theme of the enchanted princess and set in a country that resembles parts of Ireland in its grim cliffs and deadly bogs. The first half of the book has all the fascination of a horrifying folktale, but once the scene and the characters have been set up the novel seems to have nowhere to go. The symbolism comes to seem obvious and even pretentious, as the latter half of the novel gradually collapses in a cloud of inanities.

Perhaps sensing a failure here, Miss Murdoch next attempted a shorter, less ambitious version of a Gothic tale. *The Italian Girl* (1964) represents a gothicized version of a D. H. Lawrence novelette, explicitly set in Lawrence country. "Our house . . . was a big ugly Victorian rectory, its red brick darkened by the sour wind that blew from the nearby collieries, whose slag heaps were invisible behind the trees." It is filled with the sort of mother-domination, sexual frustration, and conversations about sex that readers of Lawrence will recognize. The stage version by Miss Murdoch and James Saunders turned out well because the dialogue of the novel is good and can be freed, on the stage, from the awkward interposition of the first-person narrator, a Prufrockian character of very little interest.

The Red and the Green (1965) marks another violent shift, both in setting and in technique: here the author turns to the mode of the historical novel, basing her book upon the 1916 Easter uprising in Dublin. The novel has some brilliant scenes, but it is clogged with detail and tends to describe, rather than present, its action. The plot seems excessively intricate, the family relations are too complex to remember, the characterizations slide and blur, and the form of the book remains for me obscure.

At last, in *The Time of the Angels* (1966), Miss Murdoch returns to a truly London setting, in a grimly paradoxical way. This is the setting of a

London annihilated: first by bombing, which has left only the Wren tower of Carel's church in the City; second by further demolition for a building site, with the construction postponed by legal complications, leaving a frozen wasteland; third by a thick, oppressive fog that makes vision of the scene impossible for most of the book. This obliteration of the scene is symbolic of the nihilistic state of mind in its central character, Carel, the faithless priest whose powerful abilities have turned toward the annihilation of will in all those closest to him: his daughters, his servant-mistress, and his brother. It is a fearful tale, successful and terrifying in its glimpse of the abyss beyond existentialism. It is Miss Murdoch's only truly "philosophical novel"; the allusions to Heidegger provide an accurate clue to her theme and design. It constitutes a ruthless criticism of what she has called "the neurotic modern novel" as distinguished from what she calls "the true novel (Balzac, George Eliot, Dickens)." It is the kind of novel that she has elsewhere called "a tight metaphysical object, which wishes it were a poem, and which attempts to convey, often in mythical form, some central truth about the human condition." That is to say, it is "a novel like *The Stranger* of Camus, which is a small, compact, crystalline, self-contained myth about the human condition." She prefers, she says, this sort of novel to the other kind that rivals it in modern literature: the "loose journalistic epic, documentary or possibly even didactic in inspiration, offering a commentary on current institutions or on some matter out of history." It may well have seemed that Miss Murdoch had reached the end of her career at this point: for she had, in *The Red and the Green*, shown how one might fail in this kind of documentary or historical novel; and she had now provided, with horrifying success, an extreme example of "solipsistic form" in the "metaphysical novel" of modern neurosis.

But the result of these many years of experimentation has been quite the opposite. In her last three novels, all firmly set in whole or part in the London scene, she has emerged in serene command of her own individual mode, working toward the "true novel" in the ample dimensions of a Dickens or a George Eliot, while dealing with all the neurotic issues of a society which appears "menacing, puzzling, uncontrollable, or else confining, and boring." Within this ample form she pursues her grand conviction that "incomparably the most important thing" to be revealed by a novel is "that other people exist." These three novels move toward the goal she had set for herself in a lecture of 1959: "It is indeed the realization of a vast and varied reality outside ourselves which brings about a sense initially of terror, and when properly understood of exhilaration and spiritual power. But what brings this experience to us, in its most important form, is the sight, not of physical nature, but of our surroundings as consisting of other individual men." Or, we might say, individual men and women deeply involved with the surroundings that men and women have made—and best of all, in London.

The Nice and the Good (1968) develops its vast range of characters by means of skillful oscillation between a seaside house in Dorset, where unhappy exiles gather with their problems, and London, where in Earls Court, in Chelsea, or before the great Bronzino in the National Gallery these dilemmas are resolved. This novel does not have the density of Dickensian detail that we find in the London settings of the last two; but the book, with its basically London characters, is clearly moving in this direction:

> Ducane's Bentley moved slowly along with the rush-hour traffic over the curved terracotta-coloured surface of the Mall. Clouds of thick heat eddied across the crawling noise of the cars and cast a distorting haze upon the immobile trees of St. James's Park, their midsummer fullness already drooping. It was the sort of moment when, on a hot evening, London gives an indolent sigh of despair. There is a pointlessness of summer London more awful than anything which fogs or early-afternoon twilights are able to evoke, a summer mood of yawning and glazing eyes and little nightmare-ridden sleeps in bored and desperate rooms.

A Fairly Honourable Defeat is, like *Bruno's Dream*, almost wholly set in "Iris Murdoch's London." But this time the major setting, in the area of The Boltons, is one of greater elegance and sophistication: "Feathery bushes and plump trees posed motionless with evening against white walls yellowed by a powdery sun. Pink roses clambered upon stucco balustrades and multi-coloured irises peered through painted lattices." Against the atmosphere of The Boltons is placed the decaying (and Dickensian) atmosphere of Tallis' house in Notting Hill, a step down from Danby's moldy house on Stadium Street:

> The window, which gave onto a brick wall, was spotty with grime, admitting light but concealing the weather and the time of day. The sink was piled with leaning towers of dirty dishes. The draining board was littered with empty tins and open pots of jam full of dead or dying wasps. A bin, crammed to overflowing, stood open to reveal a rotting coagulated mass of organic material crawling with flies. The dresser was covered in a layer, about a foot high, of miscellaneous oddments: books, papers,

string, letters, knives, scissors, elastic bands, blunt pencils, broken Biros, empty ink bottles, empty cigarette packets, and lumps
of old hard stale cheese. The floor was not only filthy but greasy
and sticky and made a sucking sound as Hilda lifted her feet.

These settings are admirably functional. Rupert, prosperous civil servant and would-be philosopher, lives in Priory Grove (Priory Walk), just off
The Boltons, and his pretensions are well indicated on the opening page by
the emphasis on his latest luxury—"a diminutive swimming pool which
made a square of flashing shimmering blue in the middle of the courtyarded
garden"—the pool, frequently mentioned throughout, in which he appropriately drowns at the close. In spite of his pretensions, Rupert is likable
and well-intentioned. But he understands very little, least of all himself,
his son, and his sister-in-law Morgan. His lack of self-knowledge exposes
him to the machinations of the wandering cynic Julius, whose belief in
humanity has been almost entirely lost, apparently through his experience
in a Nazi concentration camp. Julius takes a malevolent joy in manipulating
people, but at bottom his destructive plots arise from his disgust with human
follies and vanities. Here he means no more than to shake Rupert's self-
satisfaction and explode his pretensions to be a philosopher.

The real villain in the piece is Julius' ex-mistress, Morgan: she is indeed
Fata Morgana, Morgan-le-fay, the treacherous sister who destroys, in this
case, her brother-in-law. (The hint in her name is borne out at the opening
of part two, when Rupert remembers "what Hilda called 'the Tallis fantasy.'
'Morgan's living in Malory or something.' Rupert could not quite envisage
Tallis as an Arthurian knight.") She is hardly human; her state of mind
throughout the book is accurately predicted in her own description as she
first enters: " 'I don't know what I'm doing,' said Morgan. 'I don't know
where I'm going. I have no plans. I have no intentions. I have no thoughts.
I have just got off a jet plane and I feel crazy.' " But the jet plane, except
as an indication of her rootlessness, has little to do with her state of mind,
which she again describes accurately in a conversation with Rupert after she
has rested: " 'How very peculiar one's mind is. There's no foothold in it,
no leverage, no way of changing oneself into a responsible just being. One's
lost in one's own psyche. It stretches away and away to the ends of the world
and it's soft and sticky and warm. There's nothing real, no hard parts, no
centre.' " Morgan is utterly without principle, yet she is not consciously
vicious. Her trouble is that, for all her university degrees, she is not really
conscious of anything except her own physical twitches and touches. There
is much that she could have done, with even a small measure of humanity.

If she had had a slight perception into the true nature of Julius' needs—if she had been able to perceive him at all as a separate person, outside the fantasy of her own sexual delights—she might have found a way of telling him about her pregnancy, perhaps helping both him and herself. Julius is shocked when she tells him about her abortion, and there are strong implications that he would much have liked to have a son. Or she could have helped her deserted husband, Tallis, the Good Samaritan of Notting Hill, to clean up his hovel and do his good works. Despite his wretchedly poor and disorganized way of life, he is a man of character, stubborn in his belief that humanity, in all its guises, is worth helping. He is, significantly, the only person whose advice Julius will heed, the only person whom Julius comes, though reluctantly, to respect.

There is one other man of character in the book: the quiet, austere, middle-aged homosexual, Axel. From the beginning of the book he feels deep hostility toward Morgan, partly motivated by her friendship with his younger friend Simon. But his dislike is based upon a fairly accurate view of Morgan. He sees her, at first, as "fundamentally a very silly person" and predicts that she "will make—some ghastly muddle." Later, in an angry mood, he cries out to Simon: "Can't you see that she's completely malevolent, that she enjoys destroying things?" As a man of principle, Axel realizes that Morgan's emptiness is dangerous. Meanwhile, Miss Murdoch's bold attempt to display in Axel and Simon a pair of male lovers is a success unprecedented in English fiction. This success is, in fact, essential in developing the novel's basic issues.

These issues emerge exactly in the middle of the book, after the author has devoted two hundred closely-packed pages to the establishment of all her characters. This is her longest and most ambitious book: she needs not only a long space to build up the complexity of her characters, she needs an equally long space in which to explore the problem that Julius now poses, near the close of the novel's part one.

> Human beings are roughly constructed entities full of indeterminacies and vaguenesses and empty spaces. Driven along by their own private needs they latch blindly onto each other, then pull away, then clutch again. Their little sadisms and their little masochisms are surface phenomena. Anyone will do to play the roles. They never really see each other at all. There is no relationship, dear Morgan, which cannot quite easily be broken and there is none the breaking of which is a matter of any genuine seriousness. Human beings are essentially finders of substitutes.

Part two is devoted to revealing the degree of truth in Julius' cynical manifesto. He is partly right about Rupert and his wife Hilda: they are easily broken apart—but the results are disastrous. And he might have been partly right about Axel and Simon; theirs is a precarious relation, and one feels that Julius could have shattered it if he had chosen to try. And he is right about the boasted "love" between the two sisters, Morgan and Hilda: it proves empty. Far from helping Morgan as she promises so strongly in the opening of the book, Hilda ends up being "helped" by Morgan and allowing Morgan to take on the superior role. Hilda's will has been destroyed.

But other relations are not so easily broken. Tallis remains faithful to his love for Morgan; he is unshakable in his deep devotion to his miserable father; and he remains devoted, rather neurotically, to the memory of his dead young sister. And at the close, Julius rather pathetically reveals his own inner needs when he tries to justify himself and to establish some kind of relation with Tallis:

> Tallis rose and Julius fingered the door. They looked at each other and then looked away.
>   "I'm sorry," said Tallis. "But there it is."
>   "I quite understand. Well, what am I to do?"
>   "What do you mean?"
>   "You know what I mean."
>   "Oh, just go away," said Tallis. "I don't think you should live in the Boltons or Priory Grove. Go right away."
>   "Yes, yes, of course. I didn't really intend to settle here. I was only playing with the idea. I'll go abroad. I may take on another big assignment quite soon. This was just an interim."

Then, after Tallis has agreed to let Julius repay Morgan's debt, Julius lingers on: " 'Yes, well, I must be going,' said Julius. 'Goodbye. I suppose in the nature of things we shall meet again.' He still lingered. 'You concede that I am an instrument of justice?' Tallis smiled." He, and we, cannot agree with this estimate of Julius' activities. For the whole sorry tale of the disruption caused by Julius and Morgan cannot be called "justice." And the results are sorry beyond Julius' expectation: he never meant to lead Rupert to death. The breaking of a human relationship is indeed a matter of "genuine seriousness." And Julius' embarrassed efforts to justify himself before Tallis show how Julius too has been defeated, in a sense, for his cynical manifesto is less than a half-truth. The title of the novel is double-edged. Human nature has suffered a defeat in the book: Tallis is unhappy and deserted; Rupert is dead; Hilda is uprooted from Priory Grove and made to live in

California, in submission to the execrable Morgan. But the defeat is fairly honorable, for the heart of Julius' cynical manifesto has been disproved. Human beings do not easily find substitutes for a broken relation; Julius himself, as he leaves Tallis, shows the deep and genuine seriousness inherent in all human relationships.

That other people exist, that any sense we have of "spiritual power" must arise from a recognition that our surroundings consist primarily "of other individual men"—this is the great and basic theme of this recent "trilogy" of true novels. They display individual men and women in all their vulnerable and frequently pitiful weaknesses. And yet, through the quality of human affection revealed in its relation to one "beloved city," human nature finds a way of vindication and possible redemption. In her subtle exploration of man's present need to preserve the integrity of each individual being, Miss Murdoch has established herself as the most significant novelist now living in England.

DONNA GERSTENBERGER

The Red and the Green

If the "Irish" novel is obligatory for the novelist born in Ireland, then *The Red and the Green* must stand in this relationship to the career of Iris Murdoch, for it is a novel that takes Ireland as its subject—a subject approached with a good deal of self-conscious ambivalence. It is a novel written as if Murdoch had set out to explore the "Irish Question" without hope of an "Irish Answer," and it is not without significance that the *Epilogue* takes place in England in 1938, achieving physically the distance felt throughout the novel. In *The Red and the Green*, Ireland and the Easter Rising provide the subject matter, as they do for Yeats's poem, "Easter 1916," but the feeling and the involvement Yeats embodies in the poem are never achieved in the novel. This is not to suggest that Yeats's attitudes toward the Rising were less ambivalent or complexly critical than Murdoch's. It is simply that in Murdoch's novel there is an academic thoroughness, which in its determination to view the subject from every possible facet, results in a distancing from the subject that makes it forever *object*.

Still it is necessary to qualify one's agreement with Rubin Rabinovitz that "Despite a certain amount of talk about Irish politics, the historical setting is not of prime importance in *The Red and the Green*; with a few changes in background the novel could have been set in the time of the American Civil War, or the Bolshevik Revolution." The thrust of Rabinovitz's comment is clear: the Rising, which preceded by several years the birth of Jean Iris Murdoch in Dublin, provides a historical setting and an occasion for the novel which never achieves the sense of inevitability that

From *Iris Murdoch*. © 1975 by Associated University Presses, Inc. Bucknell University Press, 1975.

setting attains in fully realized fiction. It is as hard to imagine *Moby Dick* without the sea as it is to conceptualize *Heart of Darkness* set in any other part of the world than Africa, but in *The Red and the Green*, the setting, while not quite incidental, is too often coincidental. Bloom will forever wander through the Dublin streets, but his ersatz cousin, Barnaby Drumm, could suffer relocation without absolute violence.

The failure of setting in *The Red and the Green* grows not, I think, as Rabinovitz suggests, from its accidental nature, its easy interchangeability, but rather from the distance with which it is treated by Murdoch. In this novel, the Rising and the Irish are something which one has opinions *about*, and, apparently, the more varied the expression of opinions, the more truthful the novel tries to be. Although this is an equation which has worked for Murdoch before (in *A Severed Head*, *The Bell*, and others), there are certain emotional responses inherent in the Irish situation which militate against the formula of meaning through objective multiplicity.

Murdoch is quite *serious*, in a philosophical and literary sense, about her material in this novel, lacking only the seriousness of feeling, without which even the best novel about Ireland becomes a "colonial" novel. Joyce is a good case in point here, for although his attitudes about Ireland are never simple, and often contradictory, the commitment to feeling is never in doubt. The same is true of Yeats in "Easter 1916," a poem in which Yeats is much given to polemic and yet in which private feeling enters commensurate to if not consonant with the public feeling inherent in the situation.

Perhaps it is unfair to compare a short poem and a novel, and yet the novel Murdoch has written seems to mirror Yeats's poem in its general form, beginning as it does with the assembling of the local cast of characters of the (not always) "casual comedy" and running through the roll, as does Yeats, of those more public characters who are to take their parts in the transformation of sacrifice. Not only do both novel and poem work with the same materials, the questions they ask about the objective meaning of sacrifice, the terrible personal cost ("Too long a sacrifice/Can make a stone of the heart."), the political necessities of the insurrection, and the transfiguration of myth are the same. And more, a good deal of the local texture of both works is similar. Murdoch picks up, for example, the general ambience and meaning of horse and horseman, symbols which occur throughout Yeats's work to suggest moral aristocracy, freedom, daring, and mastery, and which are invoked specifically in "Easter 1916" in the naming of Constance Marciewicz, in the image of the winged horse of Padraic Pearse, and in the natural image of the living horse and rider set against the stone in the midst of the stream.

In *The Red and the Green*, Murdoch sets up, by measure of their horsemanship, an easy distance between Andrew Chase-White, Anglo-Irish by family but apparently English by inclination, and his Irish cousins. Second Lieutenant Andrew Chase-White, the only regularly commissioned soldier of the novel, wears the uniform of King Edward's Horse, but he fears and detests horses. The motivation for his unlikely enlistment is fairly simple. His childhood has been blighted by his inability to compete successfully with his Irish cousins: "This had especially been so in the matter of horses. All his cousins were natural, casual riders. They were a race of young horsemen, passing him by with the insolence of the mounted." (In case the general reference does not point clearly enough to the Yeatsian "horseman" and all it implies, Murdoch through syntactical rearrangement invokes the final lines of "Under Ben Bulben": "Horseman, pass by!") Even Frances, Andrew's intended, is described so that the reader knows her spiritual ancestors to be the Sidhe of Irish mythology: "Frances, who was herself a remote relation and had belonged to the 'gang,' [was] . . . a swift mounted girl, a graceful side-saddle Amazon, outdistancing him, disappearing." Millie, who, in part, suggests Countess Marciewicz, is identified with the savage and beautiful hunters she owns as is the only man worthy of her, Andrew's oldest cousin, Pat Dumay. (The reader should not be quite so surprised as he is at the end of the novel to learn that all the time it is Pat Dumay that Frances has loved, for no Irish horsewoman could settle for less.)

In the epilogue, the novel asks the same question as Yeats's poem, "Was it needless death after all?" and the answer, if one is to accept Frances's experience of the event, is the same as Yeats's conclusion that it is "enough/ to know they dreamed and are dead." Murdoch, like Yeats, intones the magic names: "Pearse, Connolly, MacDonagh, MacDermott, MacBride, Joseph Plunkett—And they hanged Roger Casement," and through Frances, also acknowledges that "a terrible beauty is born."

> They, those others, had a beauty which could not be eclipsed or rivalled. They had been made young and perfect forever, safe from the corruption of time and from those ambiguous second thoughts which dim the brightest face of youth. In the undivided strength of their first loves they had died, and their mothers had wept for them, and had it been for nothing? Because of their perfection she could not bring herself to say so. They had died for glorious things, for justice, for freedom, for Ireland.

The problem with giving the concluding voice of the novel to Frances is that the role falls to her simply because she is, as she says, a "survivor." She is an Ishmael stepping forth to speak to us from the vortex, and it is precisely here that one of the difficulties with the epilogue (and hence the novel) is underlined, for there is nothing inherent in the novel or in the character of Frances that makes the weight of final judgment that falls on her either appropriate or inevitable. Murdoch has, at the eleventh hour, tried to give the weight of *feeling* to her exploration of the red and the green, but it comes as a jarring note to a novel that has so carefully argued all the sides and all the possible meanings of Irish history.

If Murdoch did, consciously or not, call on Yeats's poem as a model of sorts, then it is at the point of conclusion that she is led to take her novel where it cannot go. In the poem, the single speaker, denied participation in the event itself, can make his own gesture in full awareness of its ambiguities. He writes out in a verse the names of those who have died, taking all their bewilderment and artificially simplifying it into the color of their politics. With the same singleness of purpose that the dead suffered, the poet, both setting aside and exercising the complexity he knows, writes, "Wherever green is worn," and makes within his poem a place for a consciously reductive "Irish" verse without denying the complexity of the whole. The Irish dead have earned his obligatory verse, and he, by his acceptance of his role as Irish rhymer, by his action, takes his place at their side. The verse which concludes the poem does not, however, deny the unreconciled complexity of that which has gone before, and it is the mark of Yeats's high achievement that the final line of the commemorative verse still retains the ambiguous and difficult knowledge that belongs to the *persona* of the poem: "A terrible beauty is born."

Thus Yeats's poem achieves a kind of wholeness by virtue of its coda which simply cannot be imitated by the epilogue of the Murdoch novel. The final scene of the Rising in *The Red and the Green* much better epitomizes the novel, for in it the reader is left with the image of Andrew Chase-White, the uniformed British officer, handcuffed to Cathal Dumay, hearing the confused and often hostile voices of the inhabitants of Dublin after the Easter Rising, and this is an image and an echo which underwrites the complexities and imperfections of human actions, motives, and history. Perhaps the epilogue means to suggest that only in memory transformed by human emotion is beauty given, are the young "made perfect forever," but because the memory seems gratuitously given to Frances, and because the book has examined, among other things, the destructive potential of romantic self-deception, the reader experiences difficulty with the epilogue in the context of the whole. Perhaps the epilogue as a gesture of feeling, as an imaginative statement of faith, is the most "Irish" thing in the book, but it seems as uncomfortably joined to the novel as Cathal Dumay manacled to Andrew Chase-White on that long-awaited day.

More typical than the epilogue is the general desire of the novelist to hold opposing views of Ireland in evidence. This desire results in the educational symposia which seem to take place whenever Ireland is the topic of conversation. Frances takes part in many of these, and there is nothing to presage the feelings ascribed to her in the final section. For example, early in the novel, Frances's father, Christopher Bellman, who later is to die trying to join the rebels in the Post Office, brings a report of a cheering crowd at an assembly of the Irish Citizens Army with bugles and banners:

> "But what did it mean?" said Andrew.
>
> "Nothing. That's my point. The Irish are so used to personifying Ireland as a tragic female, any patriotic stimulus produces an overflow of sentiment at once."
>
> " 'Did you see an old woman going down the path?' 'I did not, but I saw a young girl, and she had the walk of a queen.' "
>
> "Precisely, Frances. Saint Teresa's Hall nearly fell down when Yeats first came out with that stuff. Though, in fact, if you recited the Dublin telephone directory in this town with enough feeling you'd have people shedding tears."

That the novel proper is full of complexity is suggested by its title, which critics who do bother to deal with this novel read much too one-dimensionally. Typical of the general assumption is the statement of Peter Kemp ("The Fight Against Fantasy: Iris Murdoch's *The Red and the Green*" [*Modern Fiction Studies*, Autumn 1969]) that the "red" and the "green" are "the opposing English and Irish forces." Kemp finds support for his reading in the song that Cathal sings:

> Sure 'twas for this Lord Edward died
> and Wolfe Tone sunk serene,
> Because they could not bear to leave
> the red above the green.

The opposition of the English and the Irish is everywhere in the novel—historical, political, religious, temperamental, economic. It is the subject of much discussion, action, and emotion, and yet finally, with a few exceptions it is, to a large extent, as Rabinovitz suggests with some justice, the frame upon which the novel is hung.

If the novel succeeds, its accomplishment is not in politics but in character, and it is here that the title is also suggestive in ways not seen by a critic like Kemp, who is willing to read the title only on its simplest level and hence tends to see the novel as being concerned "not so much with people and their relationships, as with a central theme, the characters being chosen to illustrate this and their movements determined by its dictates. In place of contingency, necessity has been imposed." Strangely enough, it is just in that failure to find in necessity, in an external pattern and its demands, the meanings that they seek that the characters in this novel take their places in the canon of Iris Murdoch's work. The *green* of the title are not all Irish even, for in the sense that all the characters fail of ripeness, lack the experiences which they hunger after, mistake dreams of action for meaning, they do not ever find in their own relationships to the pattern the justice they seek. If ripeness is all, it would be a strange turn for Murdoch to confer it automatically upon her Irish characters because of their relationship even to an idea that led to the seizing of the Post Office in Dublin. Rather, it is in their own tendencies to see the world in the noncontingent terms of red and green, English and Irish, that the characters are marked as "green."

The reader recalls, in this context, Frances's questions about the meaning of the agony of patriotism about to befall Ireland. "What," she asks, "will Home Rule do for that woman begging in the streets?" And she concludes that she herself wouldn't know which uniform to wear, even in the Great War against Germany, shocking her auditor by her further assertion that if Andrew were to become a conscientious objector, she would "fall down and worship him." It is perhaps this exchange and others like it that make Frances so surprising in her role as the final voice of the novel which is the source of praise for the accomplishment of the Easter rising. Although it is possible that in her commitment to the Rising is meant to be the literal evidence that, by the act of sacrifice, "all is changed, changed utterly."

If the title is to be torn away from its more obvious political intentions, the *red* clearly speaks to the idea of sacrifice, the blood of the Easter Rising as well as that being shed in the larger war in France, a war of which the reader is continually reminded. At the end of the novel, it is made clear by the references to the Civil War in Ireland and the war in Spain that there is no end to the blood sacrifice demanded of individuals. There are hints that Frances's tall son, who talks like Cathal Dumay, will perhaps be going to Spain before that war is done, and the circle will continue.

The red of sacrifice is also, of course, forever written into Easter week by those planners of the rebellion who chose the Christian holy season that celebrates with the triumph of resurrection the sacrificial agony of the crucifixion. The season of Easter is spring, and the familiar dichotomy of death-rebirth, the red and the green, echoes throughout the book.

Religion, Ireland, England are the large "ideas" that the characters of the novel seek to define themselves by and against, and the very patterns themselves become ways of measuring the messiness, the unanswerable frustrations, the contingent relationships of human life against a social background. In an article entitled "A Respect for the Contingent," Joy Rome examines *The Red and the Green* as it takes place in the philosophical and literary development of Murdoch as a novelist and rather refreshingly sees it as a part of the total canon rather than as an obligatory "Irish" novel, something of a sport in Murdoch's pattern of fictional evolution. Rome's conclusion that *The Red and the Green* "may be considered one of the major works of the Murdoch canon, [for] she has successfully combined the seemingly imcompatible techniques of naturalism and allegory, thereby capturing "the substantial, impenetrable, individual, indefinable and valuable' in man, that represents for her his reality" (*English Studies in Africa* [March 1971]) pushes the case too far, but correctly insists that *The Red and the Green* ought to be read within the context of Murdoch's other work.

The characters in *The Red and the Green* may seem at first glance a more tightly woven group than in some of Murdoch's other novels, but *The Bell*, *A Fairly Honourable Defeat*, *The Time of the Angels*, *The Italian Girl*, *A Severed Head*, *The Unicorn*, and others come immediately to mind as novels with similar closed groupings of characters. The incestuous, claustrophobic, enforced relationship and the ways in which man finds or fails to find his freedom within such contexts is a consistent area of exploration for Murdoch, and it may be that the relationships seem tighter and more clearly delineated in *The Red and the Green* simply because of Murdoch's emphasis on the Irish situation.

The "family," which is a subject of great interest to Andrew's British mother, who loved to say, "We Anglo-Irish families are so complex," is quite clearly, for purposes of the novel, a microcosmic representation of human possibilities under the added pressure of a complicated historical and political relationship. (Within the family, the relationships are even more complex than the proper Mrs. Chase-White could ever guess, and when Aunt Millicent Kinnard replies, "We're practically incestuous," it is with a knowledgeable irony that makes her comment more than symbolic.)

Within the microcosm of the family the Irish members are generally shown as more passionate, alive, and sensitive than the "British" side, capable of both greater feeling and greater folly. Insofar as Andrew and Patrick Dumay embody this dichotomy, they are reenacting the relationship of their fathers. Andrew's father, Henry Chase-White, paled in the presence of his half-brother, Brian Dumay, and even as a child Andrew suffered for his father's discomfort in the presence of the Irish relatives. Andrew early realized that his Uncle Brian was "the perfect all-around out-of-doors uncle . . .

leading the way, leaping from rock to rock, followed by the shouting children," while his own father picked "his way cautiously behind." In memory Andrew sees Uncle Brian plunging with the children into the sea, while his own father sat on the shore, reading his book, forever separated from the life of nature and of the robust Irish relatives.

Andrew's fear of the life of his Irish cousins is extended to include his relationship to Frances. He identifies the sexual act with death, his own final death, and he conceives both in terms of horror and violence. His ideas about love, like his ideas about being a soldier, have been created out of a kind of British schoolboy romanticism. His relationship to Frances is best symbolized by the childhood swing he repairs for her to swing back and forth on, avoiding adult confrontation and the commitment of feeling. In fact, his relationship with her is one that he supposes he has because it is "expected." In this, as in all other relationships, he never initiates action out of his own sense of an identity beyond that of the British decency and conscientiousness expected of him by his mother. His name, "Chase-White," appropriately sums him up.

Within what seems to be almost a simplistic opposition of the reserved, sterile British and the robust, passionate Irish, there are enough variations, within the Irish characters at least, to save the book from stereotypical dullness. Health, as the general division of characters might suggest, is not all on the side of the Irish, for passion lacking fulfillment in the external world turns back upon itself in the various guises of love, and there is a certain justice in Andrew's apprehension of the family as "the snake that eats its own tail."

At one extreme within the Irish side of the family is Millicent Kinnard whose passionate nature is a terrible burden, a weapon to be used against herself and others. The question of incest aside, her playing with Andrew, Christopher Bellman, Patrick, and Barnabas, and the literal target practice in her bedroom all speak to a frustrated sexuality, a passion without object until Millie discovers Pat Dumay's passion for Ireland, a passion which is so great and so pure that he, rather than Millie, becomes the real object of the love of the other characters.

Pat Dumay loves only two things: his brother Cathal and the idea of Ireland's freedom, both of which are identified for him with death. The unhealthy narcissism of Pat's love, written clearly in his hatred of women and his visits to Dublin's prostitutes as acts of willful degradation, is complemented by his unbridled love for his brother Cathal, that youthful mirror image of himself. He must even view Millie as "a kind of degraded boy" before he can seek her bed. When he ponders the problem of keeping his brother out of harm's way on the day of the fighting, he considers as one alternative a solution recommended by its uniting of death with love:

> the thought [came] that he would kill Cathal. . . . That would make him entirely safe. If Cathal were dead he would be beyond harm, and tomorrow Pat would be free to die himself. Was that not, after all, the best thing? He loved Cathal too much to allow him to be hurt by anyone else.

Despite Pat's rejection of the easy sentimentality of seeing Ireland as Cathleen ni Houlihan, he finds in his country the dark bride who can provide him the purity not possible in mortal woman and at the same time offer him the opportunity to make the final sacrifice through suffering, to lose that gross and mortal self in a pure act of will. "His Ireland was nameless, a pure Ireland of the mind, to be relentlessly served by a naked sense of justice and a naked self-assertion. There were in his drama only these two characters, Ireland and himself." Pat Dumay's asceticism finds its perfection in death, and in its service of Ireland, a Holy Death. Ireland is the crucible in which he will try his soul. It is this hard strength, bought at such a price, that makes him so attractive to the other characters, who cannot find in the pattern of history a way to give meaning to their lives.

Barnabas Drumm is almost a parody of Pat, his stepson, and in some ways almost a caricature of Irish characteristics. Barney is a failed priest, a man whose orders are denied him because he allows Millie to enslave his affections to the extent that even when he knows she has played with him and cast him off, he becomes her creature, her fool. Ironically, after his rejection by the order, he does lead an ascetic's life, for he never consummates his marriage to his long-suffering wife, Kathleen Kinnard. He spends his days supposedly at work on the Lives of the Irish Saints but actually on a self-justifying document of his life with Kathleen. He drags out his days between the pub and the library, ridden by guilt and failure of nerve, hiding behind the elaborate mechanisms of his romantic escapes. He is, in some ways, Pat Dumay grown old, Pat without purpose, a spelling out of what Pat might have become without Easter week—without the purpose and the period of his life. The dark, mysterious currents of Irish life, which Andrew Chase-White so much fears, have in Barney been reduced to stagnant pools, although the reader needs to remember that Barney's Irishness, like his Catholicism, is his, to some extent, by adoption. He is one of those Anglo-Irish with "a strong peppering of Irish patriotism in his blood," but in the last analysis, Barney is a confirmation of what his sister, Hilda Chase-White, sees as Irishness.

If in the feelings of Andrew Chase-White and his mother toward Ireland and the Irish there is a good deal that is reminiscent of the world of *A Passage to India*, Christopher Bellman is the Fielding of Murdoch's novel. English by birth, he is an "Irish 'enthusiast' in a way which sufficiently marked him as an alien." He does not, like Barney, try to make himself Irish but rather brings to Ireland an imaginative sympathy for her history, people, and politics. If there is, in all the many "discussions" about Ireland in the novel, a sensible but sensitive point of view, it belongs to Bellman. Even though he is mistaken in believing that there will be no "trouble" in Ireland (". . . what trouble could the Irish make, even if they wanted to? They've got no arms and they're not insane."), he alone among the "English" characters understands Casement's motives. It is Bellman who delivers the judgment about Roger Casement which might well be Pat Dumay's epitaph:

> "It's the old story. 'England's difficulty is Ireland's opportunity.' Casement belongs to a classical tradition. And in a way I can't help admiring the fellow. It must be a lonely, bitter business out there in Germany. He's a brave man and a patriot. He does it purely for love of Ireland. To love Ireland so much, to love anything so much, even if he's wrong headed, is somehow noble."

Christopher Bellman, finally, on April 27, 1916, is killed in Dublin as he tries to make his way into the Post Office to join with the Irish in their "insane" heroism. The source of the shot which kills him is unknown: it could have come from either side. In the one irrational act of his life (in his pursuit of Millie he has never been deceived about her motives), he pays a high price when he attempts to join the men in the Post Office. The narrative pattern of the novel would tend to bear out Andrew's dark fear of the irrational attraction of Ireland.

The "survivors" of the Easter Rising are two: Frances and Kathleen. (Millie is still alive, "living" in the glory of the bandages she had rolled during the fighting, but she is not a survivor. She is wreckage cast up out of Easter week.) Frances and Kathleen survive perhaps because they have in common a practical concern for humanity and an ability to adapt to necessity. The cost of Frances's survival has been to make her life in England with a sardonic English husband, keeping deeply secret the real life of the self:

> She did not really think all that much about the old days; and yet now for a moment it seemed to her that these thoughts were always with her, and that she had lived out, in those months, in those weeks, the true and entire history of her heart, and that

the rest was a survival. Of course this was unfair to her children and to the man with whom she had journeyed so far into this workaday middle of her life.

Part of that workaday journey involves listening to and mediating her husband's sarcastic remarks about Ireland, which he sees as a rainy "provincial dump living on German capital. A dairy-farming country that can't even invent its own cheese." Quite confident that he and England are part of the mainstream of the world, he finds "Cathleen ni Houlihan . . . a great bore," a land of "pure bloody-minded Romanticism, the sort of thing that makes people into Fascists nowadays."

No one knows better than Frances the cost of the Irish heroism of Easter week: the deaths of her father and Pat Dumay, and of Cathal Dumay in the unfinished business of the Irish Civil War. Yet with all her knowledge, she can speak to the beauty of sacrifice, can acknowledge the gain to come out of the loss of the Rising.

The reader is perhaps most surprised to hear Frances insist to her son that Andrew Chase-White "wasn't English, he was Irish." His death had come not in Dublin but at Passchendaele, Belgium, in 1917 (and with it an M.C.), and every event in the novel seems to have made him "English," from his fear of his Irish cousins to his commission in the English cavalry. As we have seen, he had been a man fearful of experience, of the passionate life, and yet on the day of the Rising he learned and acknowledged the depth of his love for Pat Dumay. Perhaps it is his belated capacity to feel and his final heroism at Passchendaele that mark him as "Irish" in Frances's mind, but for the reader, her epithet, which is meant to be a salute, remains wholly gratuitous.

The overstatement of the Irish cause which Frances makes in the epilogue is somewhat balanced by the letter she receives from Kathleen, the other "survivor." Kathleen's letter speaks to the reality of the situation and implicitly balances out Frances's uncharacteristic romanticism. An English major has been living in the Dumay house, although now he is a welcome guest, paying rent, and an English family has bought the Chase-White house. Kathleen makes it clear that Ireland is free now but that that freedom implies an accommodation of the English that was never a part of the rhetoric of a Pat or Cathal Dumay. Kathleen's letter, which begins this last section, is not, however, effective in mitigating the romantic force of the whole section.

That Murdoch felt a need to add the epilogue to this novel and that it should seek to give a measure of distanced meaning to the events of Easter week seems strange even beyond the necessities of *The Red and the Green* as a novel, for it is not like Murdoch as a novelist to accept romanticized absolutes about historical events or to see value in such judgments. The familiar irony and distance which have characterized the rest of this novel (and the rest of the Murdoch canon) are gone, and one must conclude, finally, that perhaps in some more basic sense than Murdoch had in mind, the Irish would not be denied.

ZOHREH TAWAKULI SULLIVAN

The Demonic:
The Flight from the Enchanter

The quality of reality experienced inside the nexus of phantasy is an enchanting spell. Outside, the world seems cold, empty, meaningless, unreal. Within, it may seem neither desirable nor possible to leave. But the choice may come to be either to suffocate to death inside, or to take the risk of exposing oneself to whatever terrors there may be outside.

—R. D. LAING, *The Self and Others*

Iris Murdoch's novels ordinarily describe a psychological process that begins in fantasy and matures into an imaginative and objective response to experience. For Murdoch, "Fantasy, the enemy of art, is the enemy of true imagination: Love, an exercise of the imagination" ["The Sublime and the Good"]. Fantasy is inimical to love and truth because it is an indulgence in false images of others rather than a delight in their independence and truth. It feeds on such devices as bad faith and elusion which the individual designs to protect himself from direct confrontation with confusing reality. Fantasy therefore is itself the enchanter: to flee is to run into the arms of truthful love; to love it, as R. D. Laing has said, is "to suffocate to death." Because those who are enchanted need to see others as embodiments of myths and emotional patterns that elude their own lives, Iris Murdoch's major characters must undergo a severe disenchantment, often painful, such as that provoked

From *The Midwest Quarterly* 16, no. 3 (April 1975). © 1975 by *The Midwest Quarterly*. Originally entitled "Enchantment and the Demonic in Iris Murdoch: *The Flight from the Enchanter.*"

by a figure like Honor Klein, to awaken them out of their self-deluding
spell: "By gentleness you only spare yourselves and prolong this enchantment
of untruth which they have woven about themselves and you too. Sooner or
later you will have to become a centaur and kick your way out" (*A Severed
Head*).

What Murdoch finds lacking in the modern age is a clear perception
of external reality as independent, unique, and worthy of loving exploration.
If the sickness of the age, as Murdoch contends, is solipsism, lovelessness,
neurosis, a fear of history, and "a fear of the real existing messy modern
world full of real existing messy modern persons, with individual messy
modern opinions of their own" ("The Sublime and the Beautiful Revisited"),
she would hold that its manifestation in philosophy and art, for example,
could be cured by a therapy of perception, a rebirth of imagination. If we
fail to *see*, it is because "we are completely enclosed in a fantasy world of
our own into which we try to draw things from the outside, not grasping
their reality and independence, making them into dream objects of our own"
("The Sublime and the Good"). This need to perceive the unique particularity
of the other is for Murdoch a measure not only of virtue and love but of the
creative imagination. The contrary tendency to evade involvement and confrontation with others by fleeing toward abstract forms is the basis in Murdoch's view, not only of the inadequacies of contemporary philosophy but
also of a theory of the demonic. Like the heroes of existentialism (her prime
example of inadequate modern philosophy), Murdoch's demonic figures begin
as rebels desiring to be "free" from contingency, then evolve into solipsistic
isolated figures who pursue that unreal totality of form denied them in the
"real" world of others. Usually encouraged by the romantic fantasies of his
own victims the demonic hero becomes obsessed with personal power as his
most effective mode of communication with the inferior world of others,
and creates his own ideal necessarily out of the abstract, the inhuman, or
the "time of the angels."

In those of Murdoch's novels which treat this subject, her casual early
interest in enchantment progressively deepens into an obsession with the
demonic. *Under the Net*, for instance, is about intellectual enchantment with
form, concepts, theories, as they occur, for example, in philosophy, politics
and art. The novel finds its resolution only when its hero, Jake, finds wonder
and delight in penetrating through the illusion or net that fantasy casts over
reality. Here there are no demons, but Hugo Bellfounder becomes the
prototype for later demonic figures such as Mischa Fox, in that he is the
evasive and elusive center of Jake's and Anna's fantasy worlds. Unlike Mischa,

however, he remains an unknowing, innocent center, rather than a deliberate manipulator of other's fantasies.

The function of enchanters and demons in her novels should be explored simultaneously on the levels of psychology, social commentary and myth, not merely on one level at the expense of another. The danger of reading *The Flight from the Enchanter* in purely psychological terms (as a few critics do) is that the clues seemingly add up to seeing Mischa as a nice but misunderstood boy whose evil is merely an illusion created by other inadequate characters in order to satisfy their need for vicarious adventure and enchantment. Such an analysis, however, would immediately lead to questioning one of Murdoch's basic premises—the existential reality of evil as a necessary consequence of power. On a psychological level, the characters of *The Flight from the Enchanter* reveal such devices of fantasy as elusion, bad faith, and the schizoid tendency to split the individual into disembodied mind and deanimate body. The enchanter here is fantasy itself, that power of mind that perverts reality into an illusory, fragmented realm that can be responded to according to the momentary whims of one's deluded perception. As social commentary, the novel may be seen as an allegory of power, power conferred upon those who surround themselves with mystery and romance; more important, however, it is about demonic energy that emanates from a central figure who embodies the will to power. On a mythic level, the world of *Flight* can readily be seen as a type of Northrop Frye's "demonic human world," which is described as a society held together by loyalty and subservience of sacrificed victims or *pharmakoi* who need to be occasionally killed to strengthen their tyrant leader who is "inscrutable, ruthless, melancholy and with an insatiable will." The society in *Flight* is held together by a common allegiance to Mischa, whose power dehumanizes and sometimes destroys his many creatures. The most puzzling problem for critics has been the relationship between Calvin Blick and Mischa, a problem immediately resolved if their allegorical portrayal of the dual nature of power is seen also as a type of Frye's "most concentrated form of demonic parody" when the tyrant and the pharmakos become one. Other relevant parallels to Frye's demonic world are evident in setting and imagery: in contrast to the apocalyptic straight way, the demonic path is usually a "labyrinth or maze at the heart of which is usually the minotaur"; its obvious parallel in the novel is the labyrinthian maze in Mischa's house which harbours the minotaur Calvin who leads Hunter through the twisting cellars of its basement to his secret lair. The demonic world of fire has a brief but relevant counterpart in *Flight*: fire is associated first with Hitler, who set fire to the village where the Poles were born, then with the Poles who threatened to burn their mother to death, and later actually set fire to Hunter's hair.

II

If an abstract proposition is being tested in *The Flight from the Enchanter*, it is probably Murdoch's theory of the demonic reverberations that result from imposing restricting patterns, fantasies and myths on objective reality. Evidence of man's capacity to impose such restrictions is seen in his gods and leaders, in the ineffective organizations and human establishments he creates and in the machines upon which he relies. Murdoch sets her characters against a vast sociological spectrum of backgrounds spanning the barbaric social life of an East European village, the highly sophisticated life of the international jet set, the artificial life within a girl's finishing school, the exacting and demanding life within the scholar's retreat, organizations as different as a factory, and the Special European Labor Immigration Board (SELIB)—a parody perhaps of UNRRA for which Miss Murdoch worked after the war.

The perception of reality is defined and limited not only by inadequacies of human imagination, but by instruments and machines of communication such as the camera, the photograph, trains, cars, even the body when it is seen as an "exquisite machine," or language when it is used as an "instrument of seduction." That each character contains within himself an enchanter (the fantasy-making power of his mind) is paralleled by the connection of each character with a machine. Because the machine operates as an extension of the self, as a substitute for man's inadequate powers, it assumes the function of an enchanter in its own right.

Annette, therefore, contains within her mind the strange potential for self-enchantment, her moods of the moment acting as lenses to delineate and redefine her environment; not only can she hypnotize herself into a "self-induced coma of stupidity," she can also make a scene look as different as "if she had walked through the looking glass." Because she can amputate herself from the world through induced spells or numbness, she can at will cut off or mechanize any form of human response to herself and others; she sees her body as "a sort of exquisite machine," and sees Nina as an instrument in her attainment of utter freedom because she can be used to make herself more beautiful.

Rosa Keepe uses the machines in the factory as instruments to immobilize her feelings; unable to break the black spell the Poles hold over her, she needs to resort to the powers of Mischa who in turn uses SELIB as his instrument of destruction to deport Stefan. John Rainborough goes so far as to find himself engaged, not to Agnes, but to her shiny, new MG, which he later throws over at the sight of a bigger and better car—Marcia's Mercedes! And Nina the dressmaker is tied to her sewing machine (given by Mischa) as to a crucifix; in her last nightmare before suicide, she sees herself floating through a forest, not from Mischa, but from her sewing machines; she finds herself finally trapped by the cloth in the shape of maps of the world spilling forth from its jaws, that proceed to eat, first the cloth, then Nina. The use of machines as enchanters and as extensions of the self perhaps reaches its climax in Calvin Blick's use of the camera and the photograph as his peculiar instruments of vicarious delight, torment, and blackmail: "This is my eye. . . . This is the truthful eye that sees and remembers," he says to Hunter.

An analysis of characters as revealed in their thought patterns and actions will establish not only their psychological frameworks but their private myths, which reiterate the larger mythic framework of the novel, and will allow the reader to see how each character contributes to the pattern of the demonic human world where individual, social, and sexual fulfillment is denied. A close reading of the opening chapter in particular reveals Murdoch's techniques of imagery, allusion, theme and point-of-view in introducing us to the private and public worlds of the ingenue of the novel, Annette Cockayne.

The basic action here is one that recurs with variations throughout the novel—that of a character realizing the unsatisfactory and unfulfilling aspects of her present world and deciding, therefore, to escape from it to a more meaningful existence. Set inside a classroom of girls listening to a reading of Dante's account of the torments of the Minotaur in hell, the opening scene precipitates the decision of Annette to leave the staged, isolated world of her school for the real experiential world outside. What we immediately realize from the workings of Annette's mind are her childlike, romantic responses to the actual world, to its organizations, and to the mythical world. At setting out on what she expects to be a dream adventure, her confidence and optimism face a few of the same tests as Jake's in *Under the Net*; but the world she enters, though envisioned as the "School of Life," is a curiously vacuous one that leads her through an ego-deflating circle of experience only to return her, no wiser, to the exact point where she started just before the action of the novel began.

As Annette reaches the door leading her out of Ringenhall, she turns around for the last time to view "the expensive flora, the watery reproductions . . . the white staircase," and is astonished to find instead that the scene, though the same, appears to look quite different: "It was as though she had walked through the looking glass. She realized she was free." The ambiguity set up here is echoed throughout the novel: is Annette leaving or entering the enchanted, looking-glass world, or is she in fact carrying it with her? For it is the sudden exhilarating effect of her new freedom together with the self-hypnotizing tendency of her mind that allows her to perceive objects as if under a "delicious spell." Inanimate wood now becomes "soft and inviting," the sounds of the chandelier are now heard as "the sort of sound, after all, which you would expect a wave of the sea to make if it had been unmobilized and turned into glass: a tiny rippling, a mixture of sound and light." Swinging on the chandelier, Annette appears to be a strange waif or elfin child "completely enchanted by this noise and by the quiet rhythm of her own movements," falling into a trance and having visions of remaining there forever. The scene ends with a vision of Annette swirling down the streets of London in a kaleidoscope of colors, turning around to look behind her for fear of missing anything.

The function of this first chapter is to introduce, almost symphonically, the theme of the novel at its most basic and naïve level: the theme of escape and enchantment here takes the form of Annette's flight from the enchanted looking-glass world of the finishing school with its unreal minotaurs, its spinster tutors, and its contemptible pupils. Here, however, the enchanter is really Annette's own power of fantasy which enables her to infuse into her perceptions of reality anything from "a self-induced coma of stupidity" to a "delicious spell" of happiness. Her responses to reality provide a valuable insight into the method Iris Murdoch uses to integrate characterization and plot with theme. Thus, Annette's first response in the novel (prefiguring her later responses to Mischa) is to the story of Minos and his Minotaur. But Annette's reaction characteristically is: "Why should the poor Minotaur be suffering in Hell? It was not the Minotaur's fault that it had been born a monster. It was God's fault." What she obviously evades is the fact that the Minotaur was not "born" a monster, but was used as a monster by his master, Minos. Annette's response to the Minotaur is significant not only for its typical naïveté, but as the first of many responses to figures that are instruments of destruction, either in their own power, or in their function as machines controlled by a demonic power. Is it God, or Minos, or their instrument of destruction, the Minotaur, that is to blame? Who should bear the guilt, Minos or his monster, Mischa or Calvin, man or his machine?

Our next glimpse of Annette is her whirling entry into Hunter Keepe's office, whose tone is magically transformed by her presence. Hunter Keepe runs a small magazine, *Artemis*; the novel's plot centers on Mischa Fox's attempt to gain control, not only of this magazine, but of Hunter's sister Rosa, and various other independent "things" he can't bear to see free from his control. The tense accumulation of fear in Hunter's confrontation with Calvin (Mischa's henchman) spontaneously disintegrates under the effect of Annette's swirling folds of multicolored petticoats and her enormous, domineering smile. Murdoch's effective use of image is as carefully handled as a movie camera close-up; in describing Annette's entry, Murdoch immediately focuses on her face:

> She smiled her large joyful smile. Annette's teeth were set upon the arc of a circle so that as she smiled she revealed more and more and more small white teeth until the smile stretched across her face. "Enchantee," said Annette.

The artifice used her to reintroduce Annette as the enchanted waif is obvious and neatly done. As a type of the English schoolgirl heroine playing out her fated role of international waif-adventuress, Annette fears nothing and knows no evil; she is in fact exactly the "unicorn girl" that Mischa seems to warn her against becoming:

> Young girls are full of dreams. . . . That is what makes them so touching and so dangerous. Every young girl dreams of dominating the forces of evil. She thinks she has that virtue in her that can conquer anything. . . . That is what leads her to the dragon, imagining that she will be protected.

Consequently, her near fatal attraction for Mischa makes her feel she is in "a daze of beatitude" while in his presence: "She felt, and with it a deep joy, the desire and the power to enfold him, to comfort him, to save him." It requires the cynicism of a Calvin Blick to make her recognize, temporarily at least, that the "notion that one can liberate another's soul from captivity is an illusion of the very young."

As the perfectly enchanted product of her society, Annette never really knows who the enchanter is, and can never, therefore, flee from him. The metaphor of the train as an objective correlative for her fantasizing mind is the most dominant symbol in her life. It is the machine that has controlled her actions in the past and will do so in the future:

> Annette felt always that she was travelling at a speed which was not her own. Going to or from her parents on one of her unnumberable journeys, her train would stop sometimes between stations, revealing the silence of the mountains. . . . But she

never got off the train to lie down in the grass, nor did she ever leave it. . . . *She could not break the spell and cross the barrier into what seemed to her at such moments to be her own world* . . . the world of the chamber maid and the cyclist and the little strange hotel continued to exist, haunting and puzzling her with a dream of something slow and quiet from which she was forever shut away. (italics mine)

Within the action of the novel Annette is trapped in her enchanted "train" no matter where she goes, and though she tries to cross the barrier occasionally, her precious charms such as her jewels, the "Olympians" (the name given by Annette and her brother to their parents), her dressmaker, her photograph of her brother, are always there to shield her. When she does realize her genuine aloneness and symbolically throws her jewels into the river, she loses all reason to exist and needs to stage her suicide, but even then the Olympians arrive and whisk her off to Europe and security, on yet another train where Annette once again looks at life the way she always will:

She looked upon them all enchanted, lips parted and eyes wide. It was like being at the pictures. . . . And while Annette looked at the world, Marcia looked at Annette, and Andrew looked at Marcia.

What a splendid tableau with which to end the story of the Cockaynes! Perpetually in a state of utter inaccessibility, frozen and enchanted by the sight of the cold otherness of the other. Their unreachable beings relate to each other in what is almost a parody of Murdoch's definition of love, this unreal family whose very name, as Peter Wolfe observes, ironically recalls "the legendary utopia of the English medieval satire, *The Land of Cockaygne.*" But whereas Wolfe feels that Murdoch means to portray Annette as "an exuberant somewhat pampered sprite whose graceful innocence . . . cannot be expected to survive intact in the modern world," and whereas Byatt feels that our last glimpse of Annette shows a regenerated and wiser person, I am convinced that Murdoch sees her ingenue as among the permanently enchanted, always to remain an unscarred mermaid murmuring "Enchantee" through the ballrooms of Europe, ever enchanted by her temporarily sustained glimpses of real life out of the windows of trains, always again to return to her land of Cockaynes, "Olympians," jewels, and opulence. They are the enchanted who will, forever, as the final tableau reminds us, be enchanted by themselves, but like the "Olympians," always lend an exquisitely gracious hand to the Rainboroughs who crawl helplessly in their path.

III

From the artificial world of the finishing school, we descend to the "underground cavern" that is Peter Saward's study. Like Durer's figure of the Melancholia who sits brooding obsessively amidst the chaos of all learning, Peter is introduced working on his hieroglyphic scripts in a room where no surface except for the ceiling was left visible. The scenes within Peter's study are filled with images of enchantment and spells: his darkroom resembles an underground cavern where his books enchant him into nightmare obsession.

As the only person capable of the Murdochian concept of selfless love in the novel, Peter provides an artistic norm of the "lover who nothing himself, lets other things be through him"; having himself come close to death, Peter has experienced that mystical renunciation of ego that leaves his being free and open to the effects of love; thus, Rainborough thinks, "No man . . . had any right to be so vulnerable. . . . Here was a personality without frontiers. Saward did not defend himself." Unlike Mischa who needs to "place" people in order to control them, and Rosa who fears intimacy as a threat to her independence, Peter needs no taboos to ward off the possible powers of others. He is the only character who does not need to flee from his enchanters, with whom Mischa can feel easily at peace, and over whom Mischa has no power. Although for Rosa, Peter's love is a sacrificial gift which she can indulge or ignore at will, Peter as lover needs no protection against her power: "Stop hiding behind me, I want to look at you." Although he suffers the pains of intellectual enchantment in his obsession with hieroglyphs, Peter's relationships with people are selfless, loving and fearless.

Almost a parodic counterpart of Peter Saward, John Rainborough (who works for an organization controlling the entry of refugees into the country) is another male victim of enchantment. While Peter has the courage and capacity to risk involvement with others, Rainborough's self-conscious ego prevents any deeper confrontation than safely superficial encounters with his work or others. Both Rainborough's worlds—his home and his office—are split wide open by the entry of the enchantress Agnes Casement, whose superiority and aggressiveness eventually destroy him. That the female "harpies" who threaten his career come to represent a new matriarchy who are brighter, more efficient, and ready to supersede the ineffectual remnants of the male bureaucratic caste, perversely increases both their tantalizing charms and dangers:

> "They're furies masquerading as secretaries and so on . . . and things called Organizing Officers. There are dozens of them, dozens and dozens. They take one's work away. . . . Ravishing girls. . . . Exquisite and hard as iron, with cruel eyes. . . . They'd enslave one if they could, they'd eat one."

The pathos of Rainborough's demonic fantasies lies in his vulnerability to anything more powerful and effectual than he: consequently he is susceptible to all of her schemes, including her final one of using her MG as an instrument of seduction to get him out into the country and alone with her: "Rainborough looked at the car and suddenly felt weak at the knees. He was unable to drive himself. He adored women who could."

When the spell that he has allowed the harpy to cast over him is broken, it is not through the efforts of his will, but rather through the magic powers of a *deus ex machina*, the "Olympian" Marcia Cockayne who lifts him out of his muddle not only by ending his engagement but also by handing him a plane ticket to Europe. One wonders what realistic alternatives a Rainborough has when he finally succeeds in untangling himself from his enchanted state. Since his own reality in terms of values, meaning and purpose is nonexistent or at best ineffectual, his flight from the enchantress is a flight from what has been a semblance of complexity to future nothingness:

> Rainborough sat down. He wiped his brow. For a moment the pain in his heart seemed a little like pity. Then a great wind was blowing through him. It blew right through him without any hindrance. He was empty.

IV

Because the main action of the novel involves the struggle of characters to free themselves from the spell cast by the powerful newspaper magnate, Mischa Fox, it is necessary to explain the quality of his spell. That Mischa is an allegorical representation of power is attested to by Rosa, Nina, Calvin, and Rainborough; that he is also the supreme enchanter of the novel is implied by the constant equation of power with magic, not supernatural magic but that psychological magic which Murdoch claims is part of ordinary

life. Murdoch's descriptions of Mischa contain allusions to Minos, his minotaur and his labyrinth, perhaps to Janus (because of his two profiles), to
the hawk-like gods of Egypt, and to the Norse field divinity, the Polevik,
with its two different colored eyes.

Mischa's character as enchanter is created not by what the reader knows
from authorial evidence (which amounts to virtually nothing) but rather
from the second-hand reports of others whose reports in turn are seldom
first-hand. His power is never alluded to as an earthly or mundane phenomenon. Through Nina we learn of her own complete submission to his will
because "he bore with him the signs of a great authority and carried in his
indefinable foreignness a kind of oriental magic," and because "he was supposed to have at his disposal dozens of enslaved beings of all kinds whom
he controlled at his convenience." Annette, seeing Mischa for the first time,
feels like "someone on a high place who is only saved from vertigo by looking
straight ahead," and needs therefore to look into her own eyes; she desperately
hunts for "some charm" against the incomprehensible pain of his presence.
And Rosa, when she is ready to go to Mischa for help, is "quite ready to
acknowledge herself to be under a spell . . . [and] she knew that even if at
that moment Mischa was oblivious of her existence, yet he was drawing her
all the time." Even to the reliable judgment of Peter Saward, Mischa's sallow
hawk-like face seems suddenly to be "the very spirit of the Orient, that
Orient which lay beyond the Greeks, barbarous and feral, Egypt, Assyria,
Babylon."

The mystery of Mischa Fox centers in the inexplicable duality of his
role as evil controller and passive innocent. Although it is "current gossip"
that Mischa has dozens of enslaved beings at his disposal, yet we see only
Nina as evidence; from Rainborough we learn that "Blick is the dark half
of Mischa Fox's mind. . . . He does the things which Mischa doesn't even
think of. That's how Mischa can be so innocent." But Calvin contradicts
Rainborough by claiming that Mischa "killed" him long ago, implying,
therefore, that all his dark deeds are in fact controlled by Mischa. Because
Calvin's honesty is suspect, however (we have observed him lie to Hunter),
the reader has little reason to believe any of his statements. One wonders
whether his final accusation of Mischa is but another test for Rosa, or whether
it is an attempt to cement his own illusion that someone else is responsible
for his actions, that, true to his name, his fate has been predetermined. Just
as Mischa controls Calvin as an enslaved henchman, so too does Calvin control
his own instrument of action in the camera that operates as his "truthful
eye that sees and remembers."

To add to the elusiveness of the characterization, Mischa's public image of ruthless power magnate is contrasted with his private self-image as lonely, melancholy lover of the world. In his confessional talks with Peter Saward he sees himself as a gentle sentimentalist who, in his God-like compassion and love for all creatures, occasionally needs to destroy in order to save: "If the gods kill us, it is not for their sport but because we fill them with such an intolerable compassion, a sort of nausea." When Mischa weeps in recalling incidents of his childhood, usually speckled with reminiscences of dead chickens and dead kittens, Peter wonders "what demon drove Mischa continually to uncover and to torture this strange region of sensibility—and as he did so he reflected yet again how strangely close to each other in this man lay the springs of cruelty and of pity." Although in his own mind Mischa equates pity with love, he repeatedly asserts to Rainborough, "I love all creatures"; for Murdoch, however, pity like cruelty is a parody of love because it denies the contingency and independent dignity of other people. It is his pity for Nina, the refugee, that makes him rescue her and induce her to become one of his creatures, and that robs her of her freedom and identity until her only recourse is death. Even his elaborate theory of love, formulated in abstract, inhuman terms ("a woman's love is not worth anything until it has been cleaned of all romanticism. . . . If she can survive the destruction of the heart and still have the strength to love . . .," is delivered from the height of his attempts at god-like theorizing. Quite ironically, while his aim, as he claims, is to create a free and real woman, his means to such an end is "by breaking her":

> There is a kind of wise woman . . . one in whom a destruction,
> a cataclysm has at some time taken place. All structures have
> been broken down and there is nothing left but the husk, the
> earth, the wisdom of the flesh. One can create such a woman
> sometimes by breaking her—."

His manipulation of Rosa to aid her Protean self-revelation indicates Mischa's bad faith in seeing her as a thing, a subject being who needs to be coached on her way to self-discovery. In the Murdochian canon, love never involves the need to change another but rather consists of "the nonviolent apprehension of difference," and the delightful perception of the inexhaustible otherness of the other. Mischa's labyrinthian scheme in which he plays the God-psychiatrist intending to risk the expensive cure of making his beloved into a "real" woman, has as its object Rosa Keepe; it is her flight from the enchanter that, although ambiguous and incomplete, is the only relatively successful one in the novel.

When we first meet Rosa, she is in the process of curing herself from the effects of a torturous love affair with Mischa some ten years earlier. Desperately needing peace, she retreats to a numb fantasy world in order to evade any risky confrontation with the reality. When her work as a journalist becomes for her "something nauseating and contaminated, strained by surreptitious ambitions, frustrated wishes, and the competitions and opinions of other people," she decides to make of work "something simple, hygenic, streamlined, unpretentious and dull." Unwilling to love or to involve herself with others Rosa enters a factory which perversely becomes a microcosm of the outside world radiating its own kind of enchantment and emotional demands:

> Rosa glued herself to the machine, and the rhythm of it filled her body. . . . She called the machine "Kitty". . . . Rosa would often try to find Kitty's face. But she could never decide what the face of Kitty was like.

Never wanting "other human beings to come too near," she is no more than faintly affectionate to Annette, whose pathetic attempt at suicide is an obvious plea for attention; her callous ignoring of Nina, who tries three times to seek her counsel, results in Nina's ultimate despair and suicide, and she compensates for her failure to love Peter Saward by setting herself up as his enchanter-goddess: "The love of Peter Saward was her only luxury. She never tired of forcing him to display it and lay it out for her like a rich cloth; but only when she had first protected herself by mockery and laughter." One is, therefore, not quite sure whether or not her reasons for turning away from Mischa at the end are an extension of her usual pattern of elusion and evasion. Knowing Mischa has loved her, does she flee from him because she fears his evil and the ultimate consequence of his control over her, or because she fears the inexhaustible pressure of intimacy with a man who expects from her a passionate and unguarded love?

Rosa's demonic existence begins when her assumed role of a disembodied ascetic is grotesquely reversed into a new one forced upon her by her savage enchanters. Her relationship with the Poles reveals the different levels of enchantment in the novel, for it is here that we see Rosa's power over herself confronting the enchanters' power over her, and winning out. Rosa's involvement with the dejected, colorless, "half-starved, half-drowned animals" begins as an act of charity when she dutifully undertakes to be their protector. Almost immediately the refugee brothers' dependence upon her is complete, their respect for her abject, and their response one of primitive adoration—"like poor savages confronted with a beautiful white girl." Treating Rosa "with an inarticulate deference which resembled religious awe," they gradually arouse in her a sense of power which she both enjoys and fears. She showers the brothers with love in return for the privilege of using them to develop a secret life. In an almost Frankensteinian sense, Rosa is conscious of literally creating new beings out of the old: "She felt like the princess whose strong faith released the prince from an enchanted sleep, or from the transfigured form of a beast"; like God with Adam, she teaches them the names of things, gives them power of language, and eventually sees them using it as "an instrument of seduction."

As long as the brothers respect Rosa's prescription for the form of the relationship and refrain from threatening her selfhood with the contingent or the unexpected, all goes well. But when the brothers do surprise her by revealing their demonic manifestations of barbaric power, she protects her inner being with psychological deviousness, evasion, elusion and the disintegration of her self into a disembodied mind and a deanimate body. Her first response to their sexual proposition is "an almost physical sensation" with which "went that numb paralysis which is the deliberate dulling of thought by itself." If, as Frye observes, the demonic parody of marriage is incest, the relationship of Rosa and the Poles certainly contains elements of the demonic incestuous: from playing the role of mother, she is seduced into being their mistress, which for the Poles is not the role of wife-surrogate, but rather that of sister-surrogate:

> "You are our sister," he said. "You belong to both." The brothers
> often said this. They repeated it everytime she came, like a charm.
>   "Wife is nothing," said Jan.

Rosa's numbing of her perceptions is further apparent in her response to the brothers' weird account of the Polish woman they shared and subsequently drove to suicide; though Rosa's civilized sensibility is horrified at their callousness, it fails to express itself since her anesthetizing processes are immediately set into motion:

> She stiffened her body and crushed down out of her consciousness
> something that was crying out in horror. It was nearly gone, it
> was gone; and now as she sat rigid, like a stone goddess, and as
> she felt herself to be there, empty of thoughts and feelings, she
> experienced a kind of triumph.

Consequently, she has little trouble adapting herself to their strange sexual routine, so long as it is performed as ritual rather than as spontaneous human response, and she soon finds herself grateful to them "for the gentle tact with which they made plain to her the rules of the new regime." Thus, although a reversal of roles has occurred with the brothers now in the superior position of power, Rosa responds with her own brand of demonic power—the ability to anesthetise emotion, to cut off feeling from thought.

Like Mischa's houses in London and Italy, the Poles' L-shaped room in Pimlico is filled with an air of magic and enchantment: resembling the demonic symbol of the circle, a large empty bed frame is the central feature of their bare room; the presiding idol is their old, supposedly blind and deaf mother before whom Rosa feels "in the presence of a native god in which one does not believe but which can terrify one all the same." Obsessed with them, "allowing herself to be spellbound," Rosa watches the brothers as they sit "shoulder to shoulder inside their enchanted enclosure, looking up at Rosa"; for a while the rooms seems to contain, not one stone goddess, but four enchanted enchanters.

When the inexplicable bright bluish camera flash illuminates the room, waking them from their spellbound sleep, the light causes both a symbolic and a therapeutic awakening. If Rosa finally begins to sense guilt and evil, it is because she unconsciously feels she has been *seen* and consequently judged. And indeed she has been judged by the "truthful eye" of Calvin's camera, whose photograph is an irreversible judgment. By breaking through Rosa's fragile circle of fantasy, the photograph destroys her state of enchantment, her illusion, and consequently the demonic part of herself; the effect of seeing the photograph (taken apparently at the suggestion of Mischa) recalls parallel revelation scenes in other Murdoch novels, such as Martin Lynch-Gibbon's perception of his godmother surrogate involved in incest (*A Severed Head*), and Muriel's keyhole vision of her father making love to her cousin (who turns out to be her sister) in *The Time of the Angels*. Rosa is able not only to recognize the flaws in her obsession with Mischa but she is also made to see her responsibility for Nina's death, and to finally perceive the destructive consequences of the enchanter in herself and others.

Both Mischa and the Poles are enchanters with whom their victims eventually become disenchanted, who find their ephemeral formulas for control shattered by the unexpected assertion of another's freedom. The unexpected occurs for Mischa when the Rosa he is seeking to transform into the "real" woman worthy of his love reveals herself to be tougher and more Protean than he had thought. Able to dehumanize herself in relationships as sordid as that with the Poles and then emerge unscathed, able to confront Mischa in his bid for the *Artemis* and save it, his final triumph is in her inexplicable act of turning back from Mischa even though he is waiting for her.

It is only when Rosa quite suddenly perceives the demonic dimensions of the drama in which she has mechanically and unwittingly participated that she recognizes the necessity for flight. Her obsessive fascination with Mischa (which provokes her first escape into the factory and subsequently into the demonic control of the Poles) indirectly causes most of the tragedy in the novel—Nina's suicide, Annette's attempted suicide, and Hunter's near fatal illness. She herself escapes relatively unscathed but returns in the final chapter desperately to ask Peter Saward to marry her—a decision he recognizes as impulsive and basically false. The inconclusive ending of the novel with Rosa near tears, asking Peter to distract her lest she begin to weep, and Peter automatically picking up a book of Mischa's photographs of his "home town," leaves the reader with a sense of the still-threatening presence of Mischa forming a ghostly completion of the trio—Peter, Rosa, and the photographs as a symbol of Mischa's past control over Rosa. Although Rosa has fled from Mischa, she is still in a demonic human world and can therefore never travel too far from the enchanter or his minotaur. Her only weapon will be her perception, imagination, and the aid of her work on the *Artemis*, through which she can perhaps work towards selflessness and ward off the spells of fantasy.

In all of Iris Murdoch's novels a recurring theme is the struggle of goodness and love against the many guises of evil; the issues of contingency, illusion, reality and power are among her most persistent concerns. A psychological investigation of enchantment and of demonic power, however, is introduced for the first time in *The Flight from the Enchanter*, and reexamined and intensified to Gothic proportion in *The Unicorn* and *The Time of the Angels*. In these novels Murdoch articulates a progressively greater concern with the demonic dangers of preoccupation with form and theory. Mischa's control over his creatures in *Flight*, Gerald's pattern of authority over Gaze in *The Unicorn*, and Carel's insistence that his family weave themselves into Elizabeth's web in *The Time of the Angels*, all result from the tyrannical need to impose form on others in order that one might treat them as abstractions, symbols or objects, rather than relate to them as unique individuals worthy of loving attention.

A. S. BYATT

Shakespearean Plot in the Novels of Iris Murdoch

Literature, Miss Murdoch has said, is "a battle between real people and images." In an interview with Frank Kermode she remarked that she felt her novels "oscillate rather between attempts to portray a lot of people and giving in to a powerful plot or story." In those of her later novels where she is attempting psychological realism, free characters, the portraiture of "a lot of people," she has come to be able to make a very sophisticated use of Shakespeare, both as matter for allusion, and as a source of reference, depth, a real myth of our culture himself. The plots of *The Nice and the Good*, *A Fairly Honourable Defeat*, *The Black Prince*, among others, owe much to him, and what they owe is fascinating and valuable.

There are two excellent reasons for Miss Murdoch's interest in Shakespearean plotting. The first is that she seems to understand, instinctively or as a matter of intellectual decision, that it is a way out of the rather arid English debate about the preservation of the values of nineteenth-century realism against the need to be modern, flexible, innovating, not to say experimental. Nathalie Sarraute once remarked that what crushes modern writers is less the sense that their society and situation is incomprehensible than the sense of the weight of their predecessors' achievement, the *use* and exhaustion of the art form by the great writers of the past and the immediate past. In a sense Shakespeare, an eternal part of our culture and mythology, and yet a great technician, is available to learn from in a way that neither George Eliot, nor Forster are. Reading him can be formally exhilarating.

The second reason is an intrinsic part of Iris Murdoch's aesthetic.

From *Iris Murdoch*. © 1976 by A. S. Byatt. Longman Group Ltd, 1976.

Shakespeare is the Good, and contemplation of the best is always to be desired.

What Iris Murdoch seems to me technically to have learned from Shakespeare is, again, two things. The first is, as a matter of plotting, that you can have intense realism of character portrayal without having to suppose that this entails *average probability* as part of your structure. Real people may, do, dance in the formal figures of a Shakespearean plot (or indeed, a grotesque Dickensian one) without the sanction of the sense that one is studying a *probable* developing person in a *probable* developing society, which is so necessary to the scientific and sociological beliefs of a George Eliot.

The second is that a very large cast, including a number of peripheral people who are felt to have a life outside the plot, makes for the desiderated "spread-out substantial picture of the manifold virtues of man and society." In two radio interviews I had with Iris Murdoch, she returned to Shakespeare's comic people, to Shallow and Silence and the *particularity* of their life, as an example of a moral and aesthetic achievement beyond most of us. In the thirties and forties novelists such as Elizabeth Bowen were placing immense stress on "relevance"—to plot, to novel-as-a-whole—as a criterion for inclusion in a story. Iris Murdoch has rediscovered the richness of adding apparently gratuitously interesting people and events. These indicate worlds outside the book they are in. (A good example is the strange letters from nonparticipating people which chatteringly punctuate *An Accidental Man*, offering passion, tragedy, comedy, somewhere between Waugh, Shakespeare and Dickens; these letters are outside the central plot but enrich our vision of it.)

In these Shakespearean novels with their huge casts, the central enchanter figures, representing metaphysical powers or truths, are less powerful. Radeechy, whose death and courting of evil in *The Nice and the Good* is a little thing beside the Shakespearean dance of paired lovers, moral mistakes and discoveries, is a poor relation of Carel in *The Time of the Angels*. Julius King, the enchanter, the Prospero, the master of ceremonies in *A Fairly Honourable Defeat* enchants and manipulates both more and less, depending on the moral powers of the people whose lives he touches. He is related to Mischa Fox, in that his rootless violence (he is a germ-war scientist) has its roots in his experiences in Dachau, but his power is less than Mischa's, and the people he meets are denser. He is, like Carel, Nietzschean in his compelling vision of life as a formless joke. Indeed, his relationship with his victim, Rupert, is very like that of Carel with his brother Marcus. Both Rupert and Marcus are writing ethical treatises on Good, on morality in a godless world. Both are unaware of their true dependence on the power of the vanished religion to sustain their hierarchies of value and discrimination. Both are vulnerable to the ruthlessness and violence which mock their morality. But Julius, unlike Carel, does not behave like a Frazerian mythical god-man. He copies the plot of *Much Ado about Nothing*, and like a naturalistic Mephistopheles uses Rupert's own moral blindness and secret complacence to destroy him.

The reason why this novel is in many ways my favourite of Miss Murdoch's later works is because I think, in it, both reader and characters are drawn through the experience of *attention* to the being of others which Miss Murdoch sees as the heart of morality. Julius destroys Rupert. He does not destroy the homosexual marriage of Simon and Axel because, as we are shown, as we experience, they know each other too well. They love each other, talk to each other, consider each other, and reach a breaking-point when they automatically discuss Julius's lies and manipulations for what they are. Just as, in the scene where the black man is being beaten in the restaurant, the characters react typically, morally, entirely convincingly— one is amused (Julius), one intervenes incompetently (Simon), one makes a moral generalization (Axel) and Tallis, who represents Miss Murdoch's new vision of starting from real human needs, as well as the self-denying gentleness that can seem repellent or abstract—Tallis knocks the thugs down. This is a novel in which a patterned plot, the thoughts of the characters, the multiplicity of people, the events, add up to a moral and aesthetic experience both unexpected, delightful and distressing.

At this point it might be worth returning to the critical doubts and debates I discussed briefly in my opening paragraphs. As I hope I have to some extent shown, much of the trouble readers and critics have in responding to, and evaluating Iris Murdoch's novels, is a result of a tension between "realism" and other more deliberately artificial, even "experimental" ways of writing in her work. Robert Scholes, in his book *The Fabulators*, includes *The Unicorn* as an example of a new kind of narrative art which returns to older forms of "fable" rather than following the realist tradition of the novel proper. His other examples are mostly American, and critics who admire the work of such modern American fantasists, or parable writers, as Vonnegut, Hawkes, and Pynchon have found Iris Murdoch timid or old-fashioned by comparison. Such critics tend to see *Under the Net* as her most successful work, as well as her most original, and her painstaking efforts at creating a fuller and more realistic world in her later books as an aberration, or a retreat into English bourgeois complacencies. Political criticisms have been levelled at her for the increasingly narrow scope of her social world— criticisms that on moral grounds she herself does not feel to be valid. If you are interested in unique individuals, she argues, they can as well be located in the English *haute bourgeoisie* as anywhere.

I would agree, in many ways, that *Under the Net* is aesthetically Iris Murdoch's most satisfying novel: the balance of lucid philosophical debate, lightly but subtly handled emotional pace, and just surrealist fantastic action is new in the English novel and beautifully controlled. *A Severed Head* has the same qualities of delicate control and fusion of several styles and subject matters; drawing-room comedy, shading into French bedroom farce, combined with Jungian psychoanalytic myth and cool philosophical wit. At the other end of the scale, *The Bell* seems to me arguably Miss Murdoch's most successful attempt at realism, emotional and social—the tones of voice of the members of the religious community are beautifully caught, the sexual, aesthetic and religious passions and confusions of the three main characters, Dora, Michael, and, to a lesser extent, Toby, are delicately analysed with the combination of intellectual grasp and sensuous immediacy of George Eliot.

It is, as I have tried to suggest, with those novels in which Iris Murdoch has tried to combine widely differing techniques and narrative methods that confusions arise, sometimes because readers are insufficiently alert and flexible, and sometimes because the writer herself creates jarring effects or difficulties for them. I have suggested, for instance, that *The Time of the Angels* is best read as a mannered philosophical myth, or fantasy, playing games with Nietzsche's *The Birth of Tragedy* and the new school of "Death of God" theology. The introductory description of the character of Patsy O'Rourke, half-black, half-Irish, however, is written with a clarity, sympathy, density and lack of irony which involve the reader in a way that suggests that the rest of the story will have the emotional immediacy of *The Bell*. Patsy's actions are in fact almost entirely part of Carel's religio-sexual myth (she has to be the Black Madonna to balance the White Virgin Princess, his incestuously seduced daughter Elizabeth). The reader who had responded to that initial description has a right to feel, I think, that the author has promised something she has not performed, whatever the illumination provided by the myth.

In general, Iris Murdoch's careful introductions and histories of her characters are among her best passages of prose, thoughtful, clear, compact— I think of Michael and Dora again, in *The Bell*, of Simon and Axel in *A Fairly Honourable Defeat*, of Hilary Burde in *A Word Child*. Hilary Burde, like Patsy, is a case of a character where a change in both prose style and plotting jars a reader prepared for emotional density and realism. He is, as initially seen, a character created by education, a man made civilized by learning grammar and language to a level of high proficiency, a man of clear mind on a limited front, and violent and ill-comprehended passions. His story, though dramatic, and cleverly related to the story of *Peter Pan*, a recurrent preoccupation of Miss Murdoch's, is not the story of the man we first meet. It is an adventure story, with two accidental deaths and very contrived repeated relationships: it is a Freudian game with incest, with the compulsion to repeat the actions which trap and terrify us. It is rapid, perplexing, funny and terrible. It does not satisfy the realistic expectations aroused by the patient and delicate introductory analysis of the main character.

There is also a problem about Iris Murdoch's use of symbolism, which she herself mocks in *The Black Prince*. This problem arises more with the carefully "realist" novels than with the more contrived ones: the recurrent images of severed heads, sculpted, dreamed, analysed, in *A Severed Head* work as both joke and myth. The bell itself, in *The Bell*, seems to me the weakest part of a fine novel, because it is so much more patently contrived as a narrative device than either the severed heads or the use of the house, abbey and lake, in *The Bell* itself, to suggest the divisions between conscious and unconscious, secular and spiritual worlds. The bell is an emblem, used as such in the sermons of Michael and James: it is also a crucial actor in the narrative, and, as I have suggested elsewhere, its moment of action, when Dora rings it, is a substitute for a real action, in the real world inhabited by the characters. Dora beats it to "tell the truth"—but the truth she has to tell has nothing really to do with the bell. The connexion is the novelist's.

The English have arguably never handled the symbolic novel as well as the French, Germans or Americans—Proust's symbols, Thomas Mann's symbols, are woven into the very texture of their prose in a way that neither Lawrence's, Forster's, nor Iris Murdoch's exactly are. In *A Passage to India* Forster made his landscape symbolic and real together: Iris Murdoch attempts such a fusion in *The Bell*, with wood, water and abbey. In *Howard's End* and *The Longest Journey* Forster's symbols are rather too deliberately *pointed at* as symbols of England, or social truths (including Howard's End itself). I would argue that this is the case with the roses and painting in that nevertheless excellent novel, *An Unofficial Rose*.

The critic approaching Iris Murdoch's later novels for the first time needs to do so, I think, in the awareness that many serious English novelists are technically moving away from simple realism, from social analysis and precise delineation of the motives and emotions of individuals, to forms much more overtly and deliberately "unreal." Not only Iris Murdoch, but Angus Wilson and others are taking an interest in the fairy stories buried in Dickens's plots, in the grotesque caricatures, so like fairy-tale characters, who move amongst Dickens's more "real" characters. If *The Black Prince* is overtly artificial, drawing attention to its own fictive nature, and to other works of literature in a parodic manner, so are Angus Wilson's two latest novels, *No Laughing Matter* and *As If By Magic*. So, also, are the excellent series of brief novels recently written by Muriel Spark, which call constant attention to the fact that they are just "stories," fictions, and that that is what is interesting about them. Both Angus Wilson and Iris Murdoch have deep roots in, and strong moral attachments to, the English realist tradition. Both are writing novels which combine old realist morals, and old realist techniques, with a new kind of literary playfulness of which the reader needs to be aware.

I want to end by suggesting that a comparison between Iris Murdoch's first novel, *Under the Net* (1954) and *The Black Prince*, published in 1973, shows a remarkable consistency of themes. These two novels are interesting because both are first-person accounts by men who want to be, or to see themselves as, serious artists, and who are, in this capacity and as lovers, bedevilled by the problems I discussed earlier in this essay—the tension between the attempt to tell, or see, the truth, and the inevitability of fantasy, the need for concepts and form and the recognition that all speech is in a sense distortion, that novelists are fantasy-mongers, and that, as Hugo says in *Under the Net* "The whole language is a machine for making falsehoods."

Jake in *Under the Net* has central conversations with Hugo, who holds the view that "all theorizing is flight. We must be ruled by the situation itself and this is unutterably particular. Indeed, it is something to which we can never get close enough, however hard we may try, as it were, to creep under the net." (The image of the net comes from Wittgenstein's *Tractatus Logico-Philosophicus* in which he likens our descriptive languages to a mesh put over reality, to map it, and continues that "Laws, like the law of causation, etc., treat of the network and not what the network describes.")

In *The Black Prince*, Bradley Pearson, trying to write his *magnum opus*, the story of his love for the daughter of a rival novelist, despairs frequently in the manner of Bledyard in *The Sandcastle* about the impossibility of precise description:

> How can one describe a human being "justly"? How can one describe oneself? With what an air of false coy humility, with what an assumed confiding simplicity one sets about it! "I am a puritan," and so on. Faugh! How can these statements not be false? Even "I am tall" has a context. How the angels must laugh

and sigh. Yet what can one do but try to lodge one's vision somehow inside this layered stuff of ironic sensibility, which, if I were a fictitious character, would be that much deeper and denser? How prejudiced is this image of Arnold, how superficial this picture of Priscilla! Emotions cloud the view, and so far from isolating the particular, draw generality and even theory in their train.

(The Black Prince)

Jake has a high sense of difficulty—he has concluded that the present age is not one in which one can write an epic and stopped just short of concluding it was not one in which it was possible to write a novel. He remarks that "nothing is more paralysing than a sense of historical perspective, especially in literary matters." He publishes a philosophical dialogue, as does Bradley, who also has a crippling sense of difficulty and the requirements of true excellence. "Art comes out of endless restraint and silence." Jake is an unconnected floater, Bradley an income tax inspector who lives austerely waiting for the work of art. But both are prepared to feel gripped and driven by a sense of destiny, of direction, of a source of power, ambivalent to the last, art, love, or fantasy.

Both are measured against prolific apparently "bad" writers. Jake lives off translating the French Jean-Pierre Breteuil who suddenly turns out to be serious, wins the Prix Goncourt, and imposes on Jake a "vision of his own destiny" which entails trying to write, whatever the theoretic objections. Bradley has a conversation with his *alter ego*, Arnold Baffin, a prolific writer, whose performance suggests a kind of parody of the unflattering views of Iris Murdoch. Baffin's work is "A congeries of amusing anecdotes loosely garbled into 'racy stories' with the help of half-baked, unmeditated symbolism . . . Arnold Baffin wrote too much, too fast."

In *Under the Net* it is Jake's experience of his own misprision of people and situations, his own undervaluing of their difference from himself, their complexity, that makes him use concepts, makes him write. Bradley Pearson is invigorated by a contact with the Black Prince, Apollo-Loxias, Hamlet, the Love that is the same as Death, the Nietzschean vision which insists that Apollo the Lord of the Muses and Dionysos the god of drunkenness, destruction and chaos are both necessary to art. Bradley is wise and witty in a Murdochian manner about the sadomasochism involved in this vision of art, as he is about his own shortcomings. The fact that these narratives are first-person accounts by intelligent men makes the reading hard, since the narrator's illusions are refined illusions. In *The Black Prince*, Miss Murdoch comically layers this difficulty with references to Bradley's own fictionality, to the idea that both he and Apollo might be "the invention of a minor novelist," and with other, partial, accounts of the plot by other characters. Yet Bradley says much that she has said herself, *in propria persona*, and is clearly, among other things, an authorial joke about the relations of author and character. It is in this context that Bradley's description of Shakespeare's achievement in *Hamlet* becomes fascinating from the point of view of Miss Murdoch's work. She believes, she has said, that the self of the artist should be expunged from this work, that Shakespeare's greatness is his anonymity. Yet she recognizes, in the Sonnets and in *Hamlet* a kind of "self" which Bradley discusses in this speech.

Shakespeare, he says "is speaking as few artists can speak, in the first person and yet at the pinnacle of artifice . . . Shakespeare here makes the crisis of his own identity into the very central stuff of his art. He transmutes his private obsessions into a rhetoric so public that it can be mumbled by any child. He enacts the purification of speech, and yet this is something comic, a sort of trick, like a huge pun, like a long almost pointless joke."

"*Hamlet* is words, and so is Hamlet."

In a sense, here, we have another version of Miss Murdoch's "Good" which is virtually impossible to attain—the complete creation of a character in *words*, using the writer, but *for* the language. It is an extraordinary example of one of the high moments of art where there is no contradiction between words and things, between men and the images of men. But it is also, as Miss Murdoch and *her* character point out, endlessly comic. And Miss Murdoch's novel conducts a comic joke, itself, around the vision of *Hamlet*. "All novels" she once claimed, "are necessarily comic," just as her Apollo claims, in his epilogue, "all human beings are figures of fun. Art celebrates this. Art is adventure stories." Another thing for which one increasingly admires Miss Murdoch is aesthetic courage: knowing, better than most writers, the historical difficulties of writing good novels now, the moral difficulties of writing good novels at all, she continues to produce comic metaphysical adventures of a high order. What Arnold Baffin did not say, but might have said, in his quarrel with Bradley Pearson about being an "artist" and being a "professional writer" is that Shakespeare was both of these, too.

STEVEN G. KELLMAN

Under the Net: *The Self-Begetting Novel*

The self-begetting novel is a major sub-genre of this century. Its paradigm is Marcel Proust's *A la recherche du temps perdu*, at the same time an account of its own birth and of the rebirth of its principal protagonist as novelist. It is an intensely reflexive novel, employing, in addition to the nascent artist Marcel, such figures as Vinteuil, Bergotte, and Elstir in an effort to keep the reader conscious at all times of the problematic status of art. Reflexive fiction is most prominent in French literature, concerned from Descartes's *Méditations* through Huysman's *A rebours* and many more recent works, with the struggles of a solitary individual to create himself. Notable examples of self-begetting novels since Proust's have been Jean Paul Sartre's *La Nausée*, Michel Butor's *La Modification*, and Claude Mauriac's *La Marquise sortit à cinq heures*. Iris Murdoch's *Under the Net* (1954) is a remarkable instance of this French tradition transposed to British soil.

Of modern British novelists who have employed the resources of reflexive fiction, such writers as James Joyce, Lawrence Durrell, Iris Murdoch, and Samuel Beckett are confessed francophiles. Gallic, their orientation is Gaelic as well; each is of Irish background, thereby setting these outsiders somewhat apart from the factory and cathedral concerns of the English novel. In Conrad's *The Secret Agent*, it is the belief of Winnie Verloc, who "wasted no portion of this life in seeking for fundamental information," that things "did not stand looking into very much." This is surely an extreme formulation, but it does express an orientation differentiating French from English fiction, where the virtues of *esprit* are less often projected into the fictional

From *English Studies* 57, no. 1 (February 1976). © 1976 by Swets & Zeitlinger B. V., Amsterdam. Originally entitled "Raising the Net: Iris Murdoch and the Tradition of the Self-Begetting Novel."

universe itself. Certainly, Conrad wasted no portion of this life in seeking for fundamental information; he productively devoted all of it to that *recherche*. But his Winnie Verloc, her flaccid husband Adolf, and her idiot brother Stevie are a different story. Winnie's obscurantist declaration is inconceivable coming from Marcel or Roquentin. This is not to deny that the Künstler-roman—(*David Copperfield*, *New Grub Street*, or *Free Fall*—has been quite popular in English literature. However, such works lack the formal reflex-iveness of Proust's novel, which is constructed to circle back into itself. At the end of the final volume, *Le Temps retrouvé*, we learn of the aging Marcel's rejuvenating decision to write a novel which will recapture his fleeing life; to read that novel, we must begin again with page 1 of *Du Côté de chez Swann*. The concluding sentences of *Tristram Shandy* ("and what is all this story about?—A Cock and a Bull, said Yorick—And one of the best of its kind, I ever heard") and of *To the Lighthouse* ("It was done; it was finished. Yes, she thought, laying down her brush in extreme fatigue, I have had my vision") refer to matters within the fictional universe at the same time as they serve as a commentary on the works in which they appear. However, pervasive formal self-consciousness is much rarer in the British tradition than in the French.

Like Aldous Huxley's Philip Quarles, British novelists have been ap-prehensive about focusing their works on introspective eccentrics, who are at the center of the self-begetting novel. "The chief defect of the novel of ideas is that you must write about people who have ideas to express—which excludes all but about .01 per cent of the human race." Aldous Huxley, *Point Counter Point* (New York, 1956). Unlike Philip Quarles, French re-flexive novelists do not consider it a liability to stock their domains with artists and thinkers, a scant minority of the population at large. If, in John Cruickshank's phrase, French novelists from Sartre to Beckett have been "philosophers," it has also been possible to conceive a relatively representative study of modern French fictional characters under the title *The Intellectual Hero* (Victor Brombert).

Old John of Gaunt's "fortress built by Nature for herself/Against in-fection and the hand of war" has proven notoriously vulnerable to French literary influences, as Chaucer, among many who wrote in his mongrel tongue, can testify. Those who in recent history have introduced significant formalistic considerations into Anglo-Saxon poetry and prose, writers like T. S. Eliot and Henry James, have gone to school to the Symbolists and Flaubert. Even the technique of the stream of consciousness, the pride of British modernism, has been traced back to Edouard Dujardin's *Les Lauriers sont coupés*. Despite the infiltration of Goethe's *Wilhelm Meister* into English fiction and the example of Novalis's *Heinrich von Ofterdingen*, which, unfinished at its author's death in 1801, was to have concluded with an account of its own composition, it is to France that British writers closest to the tradition of the self-begetting novel—Joyce (*A Portrait; Ulysses; Finnegans Wake*), Huxley (*Point Counter Point*), Durrell (*The Alexandria Quartet*), and Murdoch (*Under the Net*)—have turned for inspiration. Samuel Beckett (*Molloy; Malone meurt; L'Innommable*) is their emissary dove who did not return.

The first published book by philosophy don Iris Murdoch, born in Dublin and an unabashed francophile, was an examination of Jean-Paul Sartre, *Sartre: Romantic Rationalist* (1953). As could be expected, it devotes a chapter to that author's self-begetting novel, *La Nausée*. Murdoch's own first novel, *Under the Net*, was published in the following year. Dedicated to the contemporary French novelist Raymond Queneau, the text of *Under the Net* sparkles with an abundance of italicized French expressions—*par exemple, mêlée, frisson, tour de force, tête à tête, bien renseigné, dérèglement de tous les sens, je m'en fichais*, and *au fond*. Some important scenes in the novel are set in Paris, and its narrator and central protagonist, Jake Donaghue, is the English translator of the fictive French novelist Jean Pierre Breteuil. A discussion of Marcel Proust with Hugo Belfounder has significant consequences for Jake, while Jake's description of "a suburb of southern London where contingency reaches the point of nausea" recalls Sartre's distinctive terminology. On the very first page of Murdoch's very first novel, published soon after her study of Sartre, the narrator presents himself as, perhaps like his creator, arriving in England "with the smell of France still fresh in my nostrils." His suitcases are heavy with French books.

Jake Donaghue never relinquishes the center of attention in this narrative, which is consistently related to us from his first-person perspective. Although he admits "I can't bear being alone for long" and "I hate solitude," Jake is in effect "a connoisseur of solitude," as the moving scene of him alone in Paris during the mass celebration of Bastille Day indicates. A taciturn Irishman named Finn is Jake's constant companion, even valet, but Jake treats Finn more as a mirror for himself than as an independent human being. Finn's otherness, demonstrated by his removal to Dublin, eventually strikes Jake with the force of profound revelation. Meanwhile, though, Jake declares: "The substance of my life is a private conversation with myself and to turn it into a dialogue would be equivalent to self-destruction." However, his introspective narrative will prove to be self-creative precisely through its recognition of the dense contingency of the external world.

Sartre's Roquentin, like the Dante alone and lost midway in his life's journey, is exactly thirty years old. So, just the right age for a self-begetting hero, Jake introduces himself as "something over thirty, and talented, but lazy." Jake is scarcely one of Sartre's bourgeois *salauds*. A confirmed bachelor ("It is not in my nature to make myself responsible for other people," Jake is perpetually homeless and on the move. A recurrent element in the novel is his quest for a place to spend the night.

And Jake is as rootless in his thinking as he is in his housing. A Cartesian of sorts whose first reaction to any situation is: "That would need some thinking out." Jake delights in "the sort of dreamy unlucrative reflection which is what I enjoy more than anything in the world." His tendency to examine the self, the world, fiction, and the relationships among the three is one of the marks of the self-begetting novel.

Jake gets a job as an orderly in a hospital but remains an outsider in that rigid society. "I exuded an aroma which, although we got on so splendidly, in some way kept them off; perhaps some obscure instinct warned them that I was an intellectual." Although he is a reader of James and Conrad, Jake most resembles Amis's Jim Dixon brand of roguish intellectualism. If he is a peripatetic philosopher, Jake is also a *picaro*. Throughout the novel, he displays uncommon mastery of the art of picking locks, cracking safes, and pilfering money and property.

Like any sovereign self-begetting novel, *Under the Net* has its own cast of artist figures. Anna Quentin is a singer, and her sister Sadie is an actress. Hugo Belfounder begins as the inventor of elaborate fireworks and later becomes a film producer; the scene at the Bounty Belfounder studio in which the cardboard move set of ancient Rome collapses vividly demolishes at least one notion of art. With a gesture of Cartesian asceticism, Hugo concludes by divesting himself of his considerable fortune and devoting himself, as if at Ferney, to the humble but existentially pure occupation of watchmaker. Lefty Todd, editor of *Independent Socialist*, is a political artist of sorts, and Dave Gellman is a philosopher, "a real one like Kant and Plato." But the most important artist within this work of art is, of course, Jake Donaghue, who conceives of himself as sovereign of his narrative realm. At least in the beginning of the novel, everyone, especially Jake's submissive foil Finn, exists as an extension of his creative self. "I count Finn as an inhabitant of my universe, and cannot conceive that he has one containing me; and this arrangement seems restful for both of us."

Like Marcel or Roquentin, Jake is a writer. He has composed an epic poem entitled "And Mr. Oppenheim Shall Inherit the Earth," but he is able to earn money by translating best-selling but mediocre contemporary novels by Jean Pierre Breteuil. One of them, *Le Rossignol de bois* (in the Donaghue translation, *The Wooden Nightingale*) is itself about the relationship between reflection and creation. "It's about a young composer who is psychoanalyzed and then finds that his creative urge is gone." Jake also transforms his conversations with Hugo Belfounder during a cold-cure experiment into a philosophical dialogue he publishes as *The Silencer*. In his book, which is poorly received, Jake becomes Tamarus and Hugo becomes Annandine, but reality does not submit so easily to the writer's colonizing efforts: "it *was* a travesty and falsification of our conversations."

Jake's development as a novelist is inseparable from his growth as an individual. Both produce *Under the Net*. With his literary hack work as mere translator of second-rate fiction, Jake consciously restricts his originality. But his friendship with Hugo, who serves as a kind of Quietist prophet for him, makes him aware that: "The whole language is a machine for making falsehoods." All literature, even his more serious efforts in *The Silencer*, thereby becomes fraud, if indeed "It is in silence that the human spirit touches the divine."

However, despite his philosophical misgivings and his constitutional laziness, Jake throughout cherishes a dim ambition to write a novel. From the very beginning, in the midst of homelessness, poverty, and the forces of inertia, the possibility of his future novel suggests itself. "I had contrived, in fact, to stop myself just short of the point at which it would have become clear to me that the present age was not one in which it was possible to write a novel." Much later, Jake, faithful to a still indistinct vision of his destiny as novelist, refuses a job as movie scriptwriter.

> The business of my life lay elsewhere. There was a path which awaited me and which, if I failed to take it, would lie untrodden forever. How much longer would I delay?

One of the major factors in shaping Jake's new identity as novelist is the transformation of Jean Pierre Breteuil, the French author. With the publication of *Nous les vainqueurs*, Breteuil himself undergoes a reincarnation from mercenary to genuine artist. Jake, visiting Paris, sees Breteuil's new novel awarded the Prix Goncourt and receiving universal critical acclaim. He is dumbfounded. How can it be?

> Jean Pierre had no right to turn himself surreptitiously into a good writer. I felt that I had been the victim of an imposture, a swindle. For years I had worked for this man, using my knowl-edge and sensibility to turn his junk into the sweet English tongue; and now, without warning me, he sets up shop as a good writer. I pictured Jean Pierre, with his plump hands and his

short grey hair. How could I introduce into this picture, which
I had known so well for so long, the notion of a good novelist?
It wrenched me, like the changing of a fundamental category.
A man whom I had taken on as a business partner had turned
out to be a rival in love.

Breteuil's artistic birth forces Jake to question his own neatly formulated
conceptions of reality. In the process, it inspires him to attempt to rival the
Frenchman by producing his own novel. He resolves that he will never waste
his time translating *Nous les vainqueurs* when he could be creating his own
original work of art. Ironically, as long as Breteuil turned out worthless
books, Jake was content to translate them and thereby commit himself to
imitation of trash. However, as soon as Breteuil challenges Jake's notion of
"a bad novelist" and actually writes something of value, the newly enlight-
ened Jake can no longer settle for the role of mere translator.

Eventually, Jake also arrives at some understanding of the romantic
rectangle—Hugo tells him: "I love Sadie, who's keen on you, and you love
Anna, who's keen on me"—involving himself, Anna, Hugo, and Sadie. But,
with his novel awaiting birth, he is now a new man.

> It was the first day of the world. I was full of that strength which
> is better than happiness, better than the weak wish for happiness
> which women can awaken in a man to rot his fibres. It was the
> morning of the first day.

A self has been begotten by the narrator in imagery which consciously evokes
the Creation. Jake is to be both father and artificer, as an earlier pun about
his relationship to Madge forecasts. "After all, she had no father and I felt
in loco parentis. It was about the only locus I had left."

At the end of *Under the Net*, Jake returns to Mrs. Tinckham's cat-
congested newspaper shop, which he has visited in Chapter One. Now, in
a scene remarkably parallel to the one in which Roquentin listens to a
recording of the English song "Some of These Days" in the *Rendez-Vous des
Cheminots* café (and which itself owes much to use of the Vinteuil sonata in
A la recherche), he hears Anna Quentin singing on the radio.

> Like a sea wave curling over me came Anna's voice. She was
> singing an old French love song. The words came slowly, gilded
> by her utterance. They turned over in the air slowly and then
> fell; and the splendour of the husky gold filled the shop, trans-
> forming the cats into leopards and Mrs. Tinckham into an aged
> Circe.

It is a stunning illustration of the potential power of art.

Yet one more image of birth is reserved for the concluding lines of this novel. Jake discovers that Maggie the cat, whose pregnancy has been noted in the first chapter, has borne a litter of kittens. Unaccountably, two of the kittens are tabby, and two are pure Siamese. Instead of attempting to impose the rational explanation of Mendelian genetic theory on this phenomenon, Jake is now content simply to accept it as one of the mysteries of life. His final comment, "It's just one of the wonders of the world," is an indication of Jake's progress as human being and artist in embracing the untidy dappledness of the world. He is now ready to create the work which will embody this new self and this novel vision. Sensitive to pied beauty, his language will not be "a machine for making falsehoods" any more than *Under the Net's* is.

The title of the novel, *Under the Net*, is alluded to within an excerpt from *The Silencer*. Annandine asserts:

> the movement away from theory and generality is the movement towards truth. All theorizing is flight. We must be ruled by the situation itself, and this is unutterably particular. Indeed it is something to which we can never get close enough, however hard we may try, as it were, to crawl under the net.

The sense of rebirth, rededication, and liberation at the conclusion of *Under the Net* derives from the promise of a work which will succeed in understanding the contingent world and thereby uttering what is "unutterably particular."

Early in the novel, the as yet unredeemed Jake declares: "I hate contingency. I want everything in my life to have a sufficient reason." Iris Murdoch the critic indicts Jean Paul Sartre for possessing what she considers the same heretical beliefs.

> Sartre has an impatience, which is fatal to a novelist proper, with the *stuff* of human life. He has, on the one hand, a lively interest, often slightly morbid, in the details of contemporary living, and on the other a passionate desire to analyse, to build intellectually pleasing schemes and patterns. But the feature which might enable these two talents to fuse into the work of a great novelist is absent, namely an apprehension of the absurd irreducible uniqueness of people and their relations with each other.

Murdoch's reading of Sartre suggests a view of French fiction as aseptic. She regards it as her British, and human, duty to introduce microorganisms,

"the *stuff* of human life" into the Petri dish furnished by her teachers on
the Continent.

Because of what she sees as this distaste for the contingent, individuated
world, despite graphic images of the viscosity of existence, Murdoch considers Roquentin's a "rather dubious salvation." Her own Jake Donaghue,
on the other hand, is portrayed as overcoming that orientation "which is
fatal to a novelist proper." His career in *Under the Net* is framed by his visits
to Mrs. Tinckham's, appropriately "a dusty, dirty, nasty-looking corner
shop." And, having developed an understanding of and fondness for this
reality, Jake is presumably about to become "a novelist proper," if not a
proper novelist, at the conclusion of *Under the Net*.

In *A Portrait of the Artist as a Young Man*, which likewise ends on a
note of liberation, Stephen also employs the image of a net. He proclaims
to the nationalist Davin:

> When the soul of a man is born in this country there are nets
> flung at it to hold it back from flight. You talk to me of na-
> tionality, language, religion. I shall try to fly by those nets.

However, the net trope functions differently in *A Portrait* than it does in
Under the Net. For Stephen Dedalus, freedom is a matter of flight, of escape
beyond the crippling power of nets. In Murdoch's novel, on the other hand,
it is a question of trying "to crawl under the net." Her narrator commits
himself to accepting life within the British Isles. Artistic rebirth paradoxically becomes a process of entering rather than departing, immersing your-
self in the hair of the dog that bit you. Theorizing is the enemy, and "All
theorizing is flight."

In her essay "Against Dryness," Murdoch contrasts imagination with
fantasy. According to her view, imagination, which respects the contingency
of the world, is a reflexive, provisional faculty, whereas fantasy naively
distorts reality by hypostatizing it in inflexible myths. Fantasy, rather than
being an emancipator, is a servile attempt to flee messy ambiguities for a
realm of complacent artifice. Imagination, by plunging us into the complex
mire of human existence, is thereby an exercise in free will, which depends
on an awareness that we are:

> benighted creatures sunk in a reality whose nature we are con-
> stantly and overwhelmingly tempted to deform by fantasy. Our
> current picture of freedom encourages a dream-like facility;
> whereas what we require is a renewed sense of the difficulty and
> the complexity of the moral life and the opacity of persons.

Literature, as evident in the example of Jake Donaghue, can be an effective means of accommodating the contingent world. Murdoch promises: "Through literature we can re-discover a sense of the density of our lives. Literature can arm us against consolation and fantasy and can help us to recover from the ailments of Romanticism." And *Under the Net* is a striking portrait of its central protagonist's moral progress, one which is inseparable from his growth as novelist.

Although its narrator confesses, "I'm not telling you the story of my life," *Under the Net* creates the illusion of a Proustian sort of extended Bildungsroman. The narrative is defined by two visits to Mrs. Tinckham's. When he returns to her shop at the end, Jake receives the following greeting: " 'Hello, dearie,' said Mrs. Tinck. 'You've been a long time.' " In terms of clock-time, it has not been especially long—a matter of days rather than the years usually encompassed by novels about the making of a novelist. However, much has happened. Jake's life has undergone a transformation, one that, presented in a novel, is made possible by his commitment to the complexities of novel-writing. Begetting itself and a new self for Jake, *Under the Net* avoids flight. It returns for a candid assessment of itself and the world in which it is enmeshed.

ANN GOSSMAN

Icons and Idols in A Severed Head

"Can one have relations with a severed head?" Iris Murdoch herself raises this most provocative question in her novel of that title. Obligingly, Murdoch also supplies both the myth and at least several of the meanings of her central symbol: the head of the Gorgon Medusa, the Freudian reading of such a head as the female genitals both feared and desired, and the drastic segregating of the individual from a whole nexus of relationships, to name but a few. Her characters include a psychiatrist, a sculptor, and an anthropologist. Every major character in the novel is in some sense a headhunter, with the exception of the chief victim, Georgie Hands—and when Georgie realizes to what extent she has been a victim of two brothers in turn, she cuts off her hair as prelude to a more literal attempted suicide.

Yet a secondary sequence of images belongs to a different order: art, specifically religious art. We will here explore the function of the icons in *A Severed Head* in order to show how they reinforce an ethical theme stated as a parable in Murdoch's *The Sovereignty of Good*.

"If you asked Francesca to describe her soul," Saki asserts in *The Unbearable Bassington*, "she would probably have described her livingroom." So it is with the characters in *A Severed Head* (for instance, "The room was Antonia")—all except the naïve Georgie, who lacks, not a soul, but an established nexus for her identity. The narrator, Martin, and Antonia, his wife, are always placing objects carefully "in the rich and highly integrated mosaic of [their] surroundings," while Georgie is "destined not to possess things." In front of the candles on Georgie's mantelpiece, "as at an altar,"

From *Critique: Studies in Modern Fiction* 18, no. 3 (1977). © 1977 by James Dean Young. Originally entitled "Icons and Idols in Murdoch's *A Severed Head*."

Martin places his gift of a pair of Chinese incense-burners. In the half-light, Georgie and Martin gaze at one another. Deluding himself that he loves Georgie "infinitely," Martin wisely accepts her wry emendation: "Your love is a great but finite quantity." In the light of further revelations, Martin's "love" is further qualified: he has allowed Georgie to have an abortion while underestimating the sacrifice that it constitutes for her, and he wishes to possess Georgie as his mistress while enjoying the possession (which turns out to be illusory) of his beautiful wife, Antonia. Ostensibly, he worships his "River Nymph" Georgie without giving up his adoration of another goddess, Antonia.

Yet the incense that Martin burns is essentially in honor of himself. Each ménage, both significantly lighted with firelight and candles, is a version of the Cave. In each, Martin makes icons of shadow-deities: himself and the woman. Disclaiming any sort of religious belief on his part, Martin patronizingly describes Antonia's "creed" as a "metaphysic of the drawing room" that takes the form of an "undogmatic apprehension of an imminent spiritual interlocking where nothing is withheld and nothing hidden." Martin knows that Antonia is knowingly the center of her cult; what he does not know until much later is that Antonia has withheld nothing from Palmer, her psychiatrist, and Alexander, her brother-in-law, but that she has certainly withheld the truth about these relationships from her husband. At the beginning, Martin perceives Antonia, with her greying gold hair and her great tawny eyes, as being "like some rich gilded object," which he is fortunate to possess.

Gold, symbolic of the firelight and candlelight, also symbolic of idolatrous worship, is used pervasively throughout the first half of the novel. The half-light of the Cave provides a golden glamor only gradually dispelled: "intermittent lamps lit with a soft gold the long room which . . . by some magic of Antonia's, contrived to smell of roses." It is beautiful but possibly analogous to Milton's golden Pandemonium, where

> Pendant by subtle Magic many a row
> Of Starry Lamps and blazing Cressets fed
> With *Naphtha* and *Asphaltus* yielded light
> As from a sky.
>
> (*Paradise Lost*)

Another of Martin's caves is his ancestral home, Rembers, which he calls "a superior antique shop." Here he sees his brother, Alexander, at work at his sculpture. This section of the novel bears a close resemblance to John Crowe Ransom's poem "Painted Head":

> By dark severance the apparition head
> Smiles from the air a capital on no
> Column or a Platonic perhaps head
> On a canvas sky depending from nothing;

Ransom postulates that the head (or abstract thought) that has denied the body "Is shrunken to its own deathlike surface" to become mere image, whereas "Beauty is of body." In the studio Martin looks at a clay head about to become a human likeness—and thinks of "the making of monsters." Yet Alexander wants to do what he calls "an imaginary realistic head" because, he feels, "We don't believe in human nature in the old Greek way anymore. There is nothing between schematized symbols and caricature." Here (to judge from some of her comments about the novel, her preference for Jane Austen and George Eliot over the Romantics, for example) Murdoch seems to be affirming her own artistic creed; yet in *A Severed Head* schematized symbols and caricature abound. Ironically, Martin protests on behalf of organic wholeness. Alexander has done a gold-bronze head of Antonia—just the sort of icon one would expect Martin to want. Though he concedes that "The best thing about being God would be making the heads," he mistrusts Alexander's playing God and denying the body, and he also mistrusts beauty abstracted inhumanly from "the warm muddle of my wife." A further irony is that Alexander has always been a "headhunter": he has stolen girls from Martin in the past; he will propose to Georgia; he will be revealed later as Antonia's lover long before her adultrous affair with Palmer.

The affair with Palmer, when discovered, causes Martin to extend his capacity for idol-worship to include yet another figure: Palmer. Martin supposes that he is reacting in a sophisticated and civilized way. He prides himself on suavely living up to Antonia's and Palmer's evident expectation that he will not only grant the divorce but continue to be a good friend to both of them. He accepts such a role with almost no qualms until Palmer's sister, Honor Klein, disrupts his satisfaction. Indeed, he has been enjoying his idolatry of the adultrous couple. In the "golden firelight" of the drawing room of Palmer's house, yet another Cave, he sees the embracing couple, Palmer and Antonia, "each outlined with a pencil of gold." Martin envisions them as being "like deities upon an Indian frieze, enthroned, inhumanly beautiful, a pair of sovereigns, distant and serene."

By contrast, Honor appears to be a captain armed for battle, though Martin cannot imagine why. Her first scornful attack is not upon the idols but upon their worshipper, who is deluding himself in his civilized role: "You cannot cheat the dark gods." In the next section of the novel, Martin experiences "undirected sexual desire." His turning from the images to the fire is gradual. He still sees, or fancies that he sees in the empty firelighted drawing room, some "tall shadow" of Palmer and Antonia, but he is clearly ready to move away from the shadows; his is no sudden liberation. Murdoch shows Martin entering another room also lighted by candles, "a cave of warm dim luminosity." There is Honor Klein. Always the worshipper, Martin says: "It was like an arrival at the shrine of some remote and self-absorbed deity." Palmer and Antonia have gone to the opera, which Murdoch identifies as *Die Goetterdaemmerung* (The Twilight of the Gods). Honor herself is a "subject for Goya" though Murdoch does not say which Goya—one of his titles is tempting: "The Sleep of Reason Produces Monsters." She picks up a Samurai sword and cuts a napkin in two for Martin with the attitude of an executioner. Although she denies that she is attracted to the idea of "decapitating people as a spiritual exercise," she affirms a connection between "spirit" and "power." Martin is beginning to feel a powerful attraction to her.

Yet he returns once more to his old worship, again perceiving Palmer and Antonia as religious icons. The yellow-satin wallpaper is said to "flicker" in Martin's eyes; Antonia's hair is now "faded gold," whereas the silver-haired Palmer becomes even more powerful: "like some casual yet powerful Emperor in a Byzantine mosaic." The scene is ambivalent: Martin ironically tells them they are Aries and Aphrodite, only to have Palmer retort, "You are not Hephaistos." Indeed not: Hephaistos captured his wife and her lover and exposed them to the other Olympians. Yet in *The Iliad* Hephaistos bustles about serving the nectar and ambrosia to the amusement of the handsomer deities; and Martin proceeds to emulate this role. As he tells them, he will serve them wine rather than attempting to kill them—a strange and imperfect communion, during which Martin spills wine and tries to eradicate the stain. In the end, however, he is more worshipful than ever and sees Antonia's gold head and Palmer's silver one on a white bed: "they glowed . . . out of a center of white and golden light . . . [as in] some rich reliquary or triptych."

In the next scene, thoroughly drunk, Martin stumbles down the cellar steps, encounters Honor, seizes her like a different sort of cave dweller, and fights with her physically. Soon after, emerging literally into the sunlight, he gropes for understanding, perhaps even revelation, but none is forthcoming. Instead, by moonlight, he "discovers" his love for Honor. He determines to seek her out, but when he finds her, he witnesses a "primal scene," indubitably of lovers. She is in bed with her brother, Palmer. This is the turning point of the novel. Martin's love for Honor is a terrible love, no golden illusion, but a love "out of such depths of self as monsters live in." No wonder Martin feels accursed. Murdoch compares him to a man who "has slept with temple prostitutes, and, visited by a goddess, cannot touch a woman after." Much less the dilettante than before, Martin now acquires the mastery over Palmer. Although the myth of Gyges and Candaules, which Honor later reminds him of, seems to require that he kill Palmer, Martin merely assaults him: when Palmer seeks to reassert the old authority, Martin hits him in the face but subsequently decides that the action is horrible and ludicrous, revives him with whiskey, and sends him home in a taxi. Ironically, the primitive battle wins him what he no longer wants—Antonia's return to him. Martin is by no means out of the Cave; rather, he is caught in a labyrinth. He is still obsessed with Honor even though he identifies her as potentially the image of Medusa; yet he waits for her "as a bound and stripped victim awaits the searing presence of the god." Now he is stripped in various ways of previous loves. He has parted with Palmer, for whom his "love" was only latent and for whom his reverence has finally vanished with his iconoclastic act. Next he comes upon the scene of Georgie's attempted suicide, as does Honor. The unconscious Georgie is a disturbing presence, a "terrible chaperone" between Martin and Honor, but Honor is still central. When she bends over Georgie with all of her attention, Martin works another of his aesthetic transformations: he turns the figures into "an eerie *pieta*."

"Return to reality," Honor subsequently admonishes Martin, and she warns him, "I am a severed head." In the past, she tells him, he would have sought "strange knowledge" from her by exacting a prophecy, but now he is making her into "a terrible object of fascination." As she knows, such a response has nothing to do with love or with real humanity. He falls on his knees and prostrates himself, ending in the oriental posture of *proskinesis*. Martin, who thought he had no religion, who has deified shadow-loves— all romantically egotistical projections of himself—is now completely abject before Honor, primitive energy incarnate. Only when she mocks him— "What would you do with me if you had me?"—does he realize that he is absurdly *not* "her equal." In this scene Honor snubs Martin in much the same way that the Earth Spirit snubs Faust, except that Faust has never prostrated himself.

In *The Sovereignty of Good* Murdoch rewrites Plato's parable of the Cave, in which the prisoners are in a firelit cave where they mistake shadows on the back wall for reality; one prisoner, type of the philosopher, escapes and painfully adjusts to look upon the sun. The allegory presupposes both the existence of the sun (the Good) and the capacity in the soul of man to perceive it. Murdoch merely asserts "We see the world in the light of the Good" and "if we look outside the self what we see are scattered intimations of the Good." Furthermore, she postulates not just two conditions, worshipping the shadows and perceiving the reality of the sun-lit world, but three: worshipping the shadows, turning from them to worship the fire, and emerging to accept the light of the sun. For her, the prisoners who see shadows are worshipping by "blind selfish instinct." In the second stage "they see the flames which threw the shadows which they used to think were real," and "what is more likely than that they should settle down beside the fire?" The fire is the psyche, mistaken for the sun, and "any religion or ideology can be degraded by the substitution of self." She concedes that the "virtuous peasant" may possibly escape without even noticing the fire. Most, however, go through the second stage, where "false love moves to false good. False love embraces false death." Instincts of the self are very strong; few transcend them except in special areas; true goodness is also the hardest of phenomena for the artist to describe successfully. Humility is "a rare virtue, and an unfashionable one," but only the humble man can "see other things as they are" and become good.

Very few of Murdoch's characters succeed in being good, except perhaps in "specialized areas." In *A Fairly Honourable Defeat*, for example, Tallis is the "humble man" whose goodness remains ineffectual; in *The Sacred and Profane Love Machine* the character most nearly approaching goodness is Harriet, whose apparently accidental death is in fact sacrificial. In *A Severed Head* Georgie, the most sacrificial character, goes off with Palmer, who seems affectionate but who may (as Martin believes) enslave her. Honor, still the assassin, ambivalently comes to Martin, after all, offering him only the privilege of taking his chances with her. Though he gamely retorts in the last line of the novel, "So must you, my dear," his chances of survival seem slight, and his chances of becoming good or moving to the sun seem almost nonexistent. Possibly, in terms of Kierkegaard's *Either/Or*, which Murdoch greatly admires, he has abandoned the aesthetic man for the role of the ethical man; if so, he goes, like the moth to the flame, to his own sacrifice.

LORNA SAGE

The Pursuit of Imperfection:
Henry and Cato

It is difficult to chart Iris Murdoch's progress, if only because she has a
gift for making the variety of possible plots and characters seem inexhaustible. The result of such plenty is that no new novel of hers is going to retain
its air of finality for long: it joins the *oeuvre*, it confirms the appetite (in
author and readers alike) for yet more novels. She herself would perhaps
think this response appropriate, given her stress on art's capacity to
strengthen our moral curiosity ("Virtue," she once wrote, "is concerned with
really apprehending that other people exist") but it has its problematic aspect,
since it produces a nice confusion between quality and quantity. More does
seem to mean better for her; imagination and curiosity are near akin, and
curiosity can only be fed with particulars fresh-invented each time. Three
years and three novels ago in *The Black Prince* she mocked her own reputation
for prolixity in the person of popular novelist Arnold Baffin ("He lives in a
sort of rosy haze with Jesus and Mary and Buddha and Shiva and the Fisher
King all chasing round and round dressed up as people in Chelsea"), but
for all that she gave him eloquent things to say in his defence—"the years
pass and one has only one life. If one has a thing at all one must do it and
keep on and on trying to do it better. And an aspect of this is that any
artist has to *decide* how fast to work. I do not believe that I would improve
if I wrote less. The only result of that would be that there would be less of
whatever there is." Arnold's besetting sin, of course, was curiosity.

So *Henry and Cato* offers much that is titillatingly different, and at the
same time nothing exactly new. It doesn't have the self-consciousness about

From *Critical Quarterly* 19, no. 2 (Summer 1977). © 1977 by Manchester University Press.
Originally entitled "The Pursuit of Imperfection."

language of her last, *A Word Child*, but that doesn't imply that she has somehow moved on. For her such formal questions (even self-questionings) are merely local matters—connected with the tone of the particular novel— not the permanent "issues" that they're assumed to be by many novel critics, and by pained verbal experimenters like (for example) Christine Brooke-Rose, *Henry and Cato* is a visual book, dominated by pictures (Henry is an art historian of sorts) and concentrates on the problem of making people *see* (a word that often gets italicised with frustration). It's the work of a robust allegoriser—bold, confident and unfastidious. Which means that it displays equally frankly the richness of illusion Miss Murdoch has achieved and the imperfections she has settled for.

The plot extracts sharp moral humour from the multiple contrasts and overlaps of its two heroes' careers—a technique at which Miss Murdoch has become so carelessly expert that one soon loses sight of its crude binary origins. Here, the book's beginning finds the characters at very different phases: the great decision and battle of Cato's life—his conversion, his priesthood in the face of his rationalist father's blank loathing—has already taken place offstage; whereas Henry has only just (by virtue of a car accident, also offstage) become heir to the family estate and is returning from the vacuous American job he relishes to do battle with his mother Gerda (but Gertrude [elsewhere in the book], a slip that suggests perhaps the Hamlet-Oedipus stuff in the background) and to wipe out the picturesque English perspectives he's always resented. (Henry is supposed to be writing a book about Max Beckmann, a bleak, insouciant Expressionist.) The idea is that Cato seems to be losing his certainties as Henry acquires his: desire encroaches on his priestly poverty just as Henry is savouring the dark exhilarations of disposing of carefully accumulated loved objects, and desecrating the family sanctities, not least by planning to marry Stephanie, his dead brother's dim, sexy and long-hidden mistress. Part I, subtitled "Rites of passage," gives both these developments a run for their money, tries them out, as it were (except you're left in no doubt of the reality of their pains and pleasures from the participants' point of view); then Part II ("The great teacher") with thoroughly characteristic and outrageous ingenuity produces almost from nowhere a sequence of events that leaves Henry the lord of the manor (humiliatingly happy) and Cato in a hell of loneliness that makes his earlier defeats look tame. It's one of those reversals that introduces Miss Murdoch's characters to their own unfreedom, and gives the experience of reading the queasy excitement of a ride on a roller coaster.

Primitive excitement, too, of course, and mechanically induced. However, as the structure of this book makes particularly clear, the most sensational twists of her plotting are in effect plots against plots, the author's subversive response to the designs of her main characters. In this case it's mostly done by allowing Cato's tempter, delinquent Beautiful Joe (who in Part I is seen solely as a spiritual and sexual problem for Cato) to come into focus and act out *his* fantasy plan of kidnap and ransom. So that in intention at least the shocking catastrophe is achieved through letting secondary characters (those seen or coveted only as objects) become primary in their turn, and acquire subjective space ("There isn't anybody else, there's only me" as Beautiful Joe says in Part II). The shift of attention isn't complete—what it means in effect is that Cato is forced to see that Joe *has* a reality of his own, rather than exploring what it consists in; the interest is still in what Cato makes of the discovery of Joe's otherness. But it serves to shatter the illusion of autonomy any hero suffers from, without in the least implying poetic justice. (Stephanie, and his American friends Russ and Bella perform a similar function in Henry's comic come-uppance.)

The shameless plots have, then, in the end a sobering effect, which is to do with their being a case of the impulse towards pattern and fixity turned back on itself. Iris Murdoch has always been interested in those philosophical and theological techniques which practise to know God or the Good by a process of self-defeat, and it's a peculiarly fitting form of intellectual scaffolding, because it involves in-built obsolescence, momentary illuminations (and prolific ones) which in their very nature demand to be discarded. The spokesman for theory in *Henry and Cato* is Cato's Catholic mentor, Brendan— "The point is, one will never get to the end of it, never get to the bottom of it, never, never, never. And that never, never, never is what you must take for your hope and your shield and your most glorious promise. Everything that we concoct about God is an illusion." It's a stance familiar from earlier novels; in *The Black Prince* the connection with the author's own habits became explicit, when the "editor" (pompously in character, but seriously none the less) announced, "About the soul we speak always in metaphors: metaphors which are best used briefly and then thrown away . . . there is no science of these things. There is no depth to which you . . . can see where you can make final distinctions about what does and what does not essentially nourish art." The aesthetic version of Brendan's rather Neoplatonic stance seems to be, roughly, this: that all images are obsolescent, provisional, imperfect, and that it's precisely their hypothetical quality which makes consciously—even vulgarly—*fictional* images so important. (This is a much grander way of justifying the pursuit of imperfection than Arnold Baffin's "I do not believe that I would improve if I wrote less," but tends to merge, or get confused, with it.) Cato, at the end of this book, stripped of his belief, none the less goes off in search of a taxi with Brendan's parting gift of an ivory crucifix weighing down his mac pocket; and although this partly happens to balance the opening scene where he's disposing of Joe's gun (to rub in the irony of his deconversion), it also suggests that sooner or later he's bound to understand "illusion" in Brendan's sense.

In being stuck with an unwanted icon he finally shares the fate of Henry, after all the contrasts. Henry's icon, standing in for an inherited houseful of others, is a seventeenth-century Flemish tapestry which hangs in the library of Laxlinden Hall and which reflects his progress in the novel as it is taken down in a dusty heap ready for Sotheby's (at the height of his self-confident iconoclasm) and rehung later, slightly less dusty now, as he subsides into grudgingly contented ownership. The tapestry's story, too, (Athena seizing Achilles by the hair) suggests very uncomfortably Henry's sexual surprises. However, its major role in the book is vaguer and more powerful: it is the focus for the questions about why one should cling to the texture and detail of English life (the craft may be Flemish and the mythology Greek, but the possession is English)—and about the precise depth of such illusions. To "alienated Henry" the piece of English landscape he has inherited, with its cosy conspiracy of nature and artifice, is a peculiar irritant.

> The little round clouds had gone away and the sky was an un-tainted blue out of which sunlight blended with the song of an invisible lark was radiating in glittering pulses of energy. The lake was a long flake of azure enamel and the green dome of the folly beyond was lightly splashed with silver. From the lakeside, hazy with feathery willows, the plump green slope of the hill rose towards the wood. The wind had dropped and over the rounded heads of the now quiet trees rose the radiant pale grey tower of Dimmerstone church. Henry looked at it all, and it was like looking at his own mind, his own being, perhaps his only reality. So much the worse for reality then, as thought; and an old favourite Latin tag came to him out of his boyhood. *Solitudinem facio, pacem appello*. No, no one at the Hall was laughing, Henry had seen to that. It must all be destroyed, all rolled up like a tapestry.

The view *is* like a tapestry, mere "stuff" elaborated, "all a kind of illusion" in the habits and the values it represents, and yet (as Henry here is realising; he's on the brink of reversing his destructive edicts) without it the sense of his own separate identity would be lost. It's only in relation to these shame-fully picturesque details that his particular moral style has come into exis-tence; when virginal and dangerous Colette emerges from the landscape to claim him (like Athena) it's less to do with abstract mythological passions than with a very local destiny. In planning to marry ex-whore Stephanie (who anyway turns out to have been a failed typist with a colourful fantasy life) and in admiring Max Beckmann's harlequins, Henry was trying for a kind of impersonal freedom that can't exist in Iris Murdoch's world. His tapestry (and the same is true of Cato's crucifix) is to do with accepting the particular object—the particular, provisional vision—that happens to belong to you.

The descriptive strength of *Henry and Cato* reaffirms the importance for her of *picturing* the variousness of people's lives and landscapes. Lives that cannot be pictured hardly exist; there is a character in *The Nice and the Good* (1968), Jessica, who "had never developed the faculty of colouring and structuring her surroundings into a moral habitation, the faculty which is sometimes called "moral sense," but she gets drawn into the imaginable world by the end. The bleakest scenes from provincial life acquire an inverted style, as when Bradley in *The Black Prince* reflects on his sister's flimsy marriage, "there was a kind of fairly solid ordinariness about that 'maisonette' in Bristol, with its expensive kitchen equipment and its horrible modern cutlery, and the imitation 'bar' in the corner of the drawing room. Even the stupider vanities of the modern world can have a kind of innocence, a sort of anchoring, steadying quality." When her marriage breaks up Priscilla dies for want of the pathetic list of "things" ("And the little ornaments, that stripey vase . . .") in which her identity inheres. In *An Accidental Man* (1971) Charlotte finds herself similarly disinherited: "She owned her tooth-brush but not the mug in which it stood . . . Everything was entirely as usual, and yet utterly alienated, as if what one had taken to be someone's house had turned out to be an antique shop. Just for a moment all these things were proclaiming a secret truth . . . Ownership was an illusion." It's an illusion one can hardly live without, however; in *Henry and Cato* the most telling instance of a life-style is Cato's—he believes himself to have given up the world, but the descriptions of his condemned "Mission" off the seedy end of Ladbroke Grove are just as suggestive of the tug of things as the tapestry-texture of Henry's estate:

He took off his macintosh and propped his streaming umbrella in a corner, whence a rivulet proceeded across the floor making pools in the cracked tiles and disturbing a gathering of the semi-transparent beetles who were now shameless inhabitants of the kitchen.

The dim light showed, immediateley outside the door, the steep stairs which Cato now mounted to the room above where he once more checked the window which had been partially boarded up and more recently covered by a blanket hung from two nails . . . There was a chest of drawers with the drawers standing open and empty, a divan bed with a dirty flimsy green coverlet drawn up over disorderly bedclothes, and a small metal crucifix nailed to the wall above. . . . There were two upright chairs and a number of overflowing ashtrays. The room smelt of damp and tobacco and the lavatory next door.

This loving inventory brings out just how cumbered you can be when you have, in theory, nothing; decorum reigns here too, with "semi-transparent beetles" instead of larks, and "overflowing ashtrays" instead of "big Italian vases." The scene has a pictorial quiet and stasis that places Cato and articulates his identity, especially his unfreedom.

Not surprisingly for a book so visually conceived, *Henry and Cato* imagines hell as sensory deprivation. Conned by Joe into thinking he has been kidnapped by a gang, Cato finds himself locked in total darkness in what turns out to be an old air-raid shelter, and there, truly stripped of possessions, he falls apart—"it was not exactly like going mad, it was more like a gentle disintegration of a tentacular thought stuff . . . which now floated quietly away into the dark." And though the chain of events which leads him to draw his sister into the trap, and to kill Joe, is not of his own making, the fear and violence he displays truly reveal him to himself. Or rather, reveal how little there is of him, and how horrible that little is, when he is deprived of the circumstantial details of his existence. Moral existence is a matter of detailed images, without those illusory points of reference people die. *The Nice and the Good*, another novel full of pictorial detail, also used deep shelters under London (and a tide-filled cave) to demonstrate the fragility of mental space unsupported by the colours and perspectives of the art of material life. In Iris Murdoch's world it is spiritual arrogance of the most dangerous kind to suppose that you can become cultureless; she is not much troubled by the snobbish imperative of placing the quality of one kind of life over another, but she refuses to imagine a life that is "free" of cultural patterns.

Which brings one back to the question of the peculiar kind of illusion her novels are after. She has, at least since *The Nice and the Good* in 1968, settled into a confident formula which stresses both the richness of detail and its disposability ("metaphors . . . used briefly and then thrown away"). Presumably it works so well because it feeds the moral curiosity about "otherness" without subjecting any one set of characters to the kind of intense scrutiny that might merge them with the author. She no longer seems (if she ever did) interested in building a symbolic system or making a myth: her basic procedure is a loose form of allegory (or allegorising, to emphasise that it's a continuous process) and her mythological figures are deliberately attached to particular pieces of canvas, as though she is insisting on their being human creations. She has depth, but like the depth of her favourite paintings it is limited, and illusory (in the sense that you're meant to accept it as an approximation). Her treatment of minor characters—those not directly necessary to the action, who by their gratuitous presence seem especially to show "that other people exist"—is interestingly similar to the arrangements of perspective in painting:

> Henry . . . was in the National Gallery, examining the most important acquisition made during his absence, Titian's great *Diana and Actaeon*. The immortal goddess, with curving apple cheek, her bow uplifted, bounds with graceful ruthless indifference across the foreground, while further back, in an underworld of brooding light, the doll-like figure of Actaeon falls stiffly to the onslaught of the dogs. A stream flashes. A mysterious horseman passes. The woods, the air, are of a russet brown so intense and frightening as to persuade one that the tragedy is taking place in total silence.

Henry takes it rather smugly as a reminder of the dangerous forces that toy with human destinies, but his own happy ending will prove him wrong. The forces at work in his world, while no less mysterious, are thoroughly human. What he should have paid attention to was the eerie mutual ignorance of the figures in the painting—Diana in the foreground, Actaeon dying in his underworld, the horseman in the distance. It's this ignorance, this living in separate worlds, that seems to Iris Murdoch to pose the central problems in both art and morality. And while a painting, or a novel, can seem to face and overcome our blindness, they share in it too. The "mysterious horseman"—the minor character—on the skyline has to stand in for the endless variety of other lives and possibilities that lie beyond. One way of taking an allegory is to see in it a universal image, on which individual dilemmas converge; Miss Murdoch seems to see it rather differently, as a way of expressing the provisional nature of one's world picture. Her minor characters are, in their stylised "realism," a measure of the scepticism she permits herself about her fictional world.

In *Henry and Cato*, Lucius Lamb plays the role of minor character, being visible to author and readers, but for the most part invisible to the main protagonists. Lucius, an aged beautiful youth, a writer whose ambition has shrunk from the great work on Marxism to absurd haiku, and whose life has become devoted to a spooky and rather cowardly attendance on robust Gerda, is a horribly sympathetic and funny creation. The insight one's given into his weary, self-centred but not always silly reflections, contrasted with the irritable callousness with which he's regarded by the others (when they notice him at all) provides an extremely effective variation on the book's theme. And his lonely death, which like everything else in his life takes him somehow by surprise, heralds the book's ending and final horizon, as in "a strange scrawling hand" he writes his last haiku. "So many dawns I was blind to. / Now the illumination of night / Comes to me too late, O great teacher." Its feeble truth sums up with tragicomic fitness the ironies of his shadowy career. He has his "otherness," his separate being, but he is on the very verge of visibility, fading as if by his own volition (except that we know he didn't wish it at all) into anonymity. Beyond him there are only joke characters like "Giles Gosling the architect" who is much talked of but never appears, and Rhoda the maid at the Hall whose speech defect makes her unintelligible to all except Gerda (and Lucius when he's dying) and who is revealed at the last moment to have played a significant part in securing oblivious Henry's inheritance.

With Rhoda, one arrives at Miss Murdoch's outer space, which she has from time to time adumbrated by talking about people in other dimensions, and "sightings": in *The Nice and the Good* some high-powered binoculars are used to help out people's short-sightedness, and the twins see a flying saucer; in *The Sacred and Profane Love Machine* the mysterious cupid in Titian's painting turns into the even more mysterious Luca, who seems to have a higher specific gravity than the other characters, and who becomes speechless and is shut up in an institution. It's tempting to see these glimpses of alien life—these vanishing points—as the objects of her fictional quest, when one recalls the stress in her critical writings on the value of "contingency." However, as the novel's humour on this topic makes clear, she has no time for such literal-minded, doomed researches. She does not attempt to convey the absolute density, chanciness and impenetrability of life; probably she considers that such an attempt would be self-defeating, because it would involve a degree of stylistic self-consciousness, and narcissism, which would after all lose sight of the object. (This seems to be her largest doubt about modernist writers in her early book on Sartre.) Instead she settles for the illusion of a three-dimensional moral world, achieved through her own particular adaptation or rather traditional fictional techniques. None of her novels dwells exhaustively on its subjects, or on its own language. The imaginative curiosity that is always left over feeds into a new book.

Her aesthetic of imperfection is powerfully attractive because it mocks the critical demand for totalities, and makes fiction seem a living process. There is still a distinction to be made, though, between the allegorising shortcuts which belong to her special kind of novel, and the casual signs of haste and writing by formula which beset her. *Henry and Cato* has more than its share of these, along with its dashing, elaborate design. The opening twenty-odd pages, for example, are liberally dotted with formulae like "lost Henry," "refugee Henry," "tactless Henry," "creep Lamb," "up-early Bella," "semi-educated Sandy," and so on, which die out later without having performed any obviously useful function. And more seriously, the novel's two dangerous young people, Cato's Beautiful Joe, and Henry's virgin pursuer Colette, whose entries on to centre stage in Part II reverse and resolve the plot, both remain sketchy and emblematic. Especially Colette, who is talked of as a "virgin knight" and seems to be modelled on Spenser's magical virgins, but lacks their erotic presence. The effect on the book's structure is that there's an emblematic blur in the middle distance: it doesn't destroy the sense of depth, although it does make it seem too facilely achieved. This sort of thing doesn't demonstrate that she should write less, either—merely that she risks a great deal by following her instincts about the pace of her work. There is no other contemporary British novelist whose habitual expertise one can trust in so much.

DOROTHY A. WINSOR

Solipsistic Sexuality in Murdoch's Gothic Novels

One of Iris Murdoch's central preoccupations as both philosopher and novelist is the relationship between man's inner world of drives and fantasies and the outer world of social structure and other people. She believes that man naturally sees the world through the distorting glass of his own desires and only gradually, through contact with exterior reality, learns to modify his views. For Murdoch, this modification is a moral action: ". . . Goodness," she writes, "is a form of realism" which prevents us from "living in a private dream world" and disregarding the obligations imposed by the world around us. Respect for the exterior world, however, is difficult for Murdoch's characters to achieve. This is shown most importantly by their tendency to misperceive the world according to their fantasies, but it is epitomized in their sexual relationships. With almost monotonous regularity, those relationships reflect a denial of the separate reality of the other. They are attempts to merge with and become the other, or incestuous or homosexual love for what is most like the self, or sadomasochistic denials of the dignity of one partner. They seldom express that recognition of and respect for another, that "discovery of reality," which Murdoch identifies with love. In her study of Plato, Murdoch implies that she shares his idea of eros, or transformed sexual energy, as a prime force, leading one to reach out of the self to the rest of the world, but in her novels, sexual energy more often remains a drive characters seek to satisfy in self-absorbed ways.

Murdoch's experiments with Gothic conventions are an exploration of the tension between inner and outer world and its expression in sexuality.

From *Renascence* 34, no. 1 (Autumn 1981). © 1981 by *Renascence*. Originally entitled "Solipsistic Sexuality in Iris Murdoch's Gothic Novels."

Gothic conventions traditionally focus upon the inner world, isolating characters from any other. The outer world of society, for instance, is limited
to the self-absorbed sexual relationships described above, and the outer world
of nature exists only as a reflection of the central character's feelings. Within
this isolated setting, characters act out desires whose pre-socialized nature
is indicated by their link with ancient times and legend. Murdoch has always
used some Gothic motifs, but they appear in her novels with increased
frequency between 1958 and 1966. *The Unicorn* (1963) and *The Time of the
Angels* (1966) are fully-fledged Gothic novels, and *The Bell* (1958) has a
strong Gothic subplot. Using these conventions, Murdoch portrays the
dangers of this solipsistic world view and examines the possibilities for
transformation of its primitive sexuality into eros. The possibility for transformation is most optimistically upheld in *The Bell*, whose publication initiates her Gothic period. As she moves from *The Bell* to *The Unicorn* to *The
Time of the Angels*, however, sexuality becomes more and more dangerous
and love becomes less and less possible. It is as though in the first novel
passion is always potentially transformable to love, while in the later books
love is always in danger of disintegrating into self-absorbed passion. With
her next novel, *The Nice and the Good* (1968), Murdoch ceases to write Gothic
novels. She uses occasional Gothic motifs in subsequent novels, but she never
again portrays a Gothic world. I should like to explore, as no one has yet
done, Murdoch's shifting views of the potential of Gothic sexuality which
finally lead to her repudiation of the form. (Zohreh T. Sullivan . . . treats
the growing solipsism of Murdoch's Gothic novels, but she excludes *The
Bell* and does not account for Murdoch's ceasing to write them.)

In *The Bell*, Murdoch manipulates the central Gothic element of the
nunnery to suggest that the denial of inner drives prevents their transformation and is thus an enemy of love. Most of the characters are members
of Imber Court, a lay religious community. Their relationship to their
passions is symbolized by the relationship of the Court to Imber Abbey,
which is always in the background and yet is separated from the Court by
a lake. The characters associate the Abbey, like the Gothic convent or
monastery, with buried and imprisoned impulses, with "evil" "in the depths
of [the] mind." The link between the Abbey and primitive passions is
reinforced by the Abbey's legend of the bell. In the legend, when a nun
with a lover proved unrepentant, the bell in the Abbey tower leaped from
its place and hurled itself into the lake. Overwhelmed by this display, the
nun, too, hurled herself into the water and was drowned. Through this
legend and the traditional Gothic role of the convent, the Abbey becomes
a symbol of passion from which the inhabitants of Imber court attempt to

distance themselves. In the course of the novel, Dora and Toby, visitors to the Court, find the old bell on the bottom of the lake and drag it to the surface. As it emerges from the lake, the repressed passions it represents emerge and demand attention.

Imber Court's original attitude toward primitive drives is typified by member James Tayper Pace, who ignores any tales of an ancient bell and talks instead of a new bell the Abbey has purchased. James uses the ringing of the new bell to represent innocence and candor, epitomizing his idea of virtue. For James, goodness results from living by plain rules given by a sovereign God. His religion is thus a force which prevents self-created fantasies but which, by definition, cannot give James knowledge of the inner life of himself and others. James's ignorance leaves him unintentionally unloving and destructive, as is most evident in his sharing of the community's distorted idea of Catherine Fawley.

James describes the community's picture of Catherine when he compares her to the new bell, his symbol of innocence, She has, however, been involved in an incestuous love for her twin brother, Nick. Catherine and Nick's twinship, their resemblance to one another, and their mutual love for Court leader, Michael Meade, emphasize the solipsistic nature of their love. Despite their sameness, however, the natures Catherine and Nick exhibit to the community fit the highly differentiated male-female stereotypes common in Gothic fiction: the community sees Catherine as all pure and Nick as debauched and defiant. As the new bell, then, has in the old bell a twin associated with passion, Catherine, who has been compared to the new bell, has a twin in Nick. The denial of this element in her, which the Court encourages, has serious consequences, as her attempted suicide and subsequent dementia attest. James has compared Catherine to the new bell, and when she believes the new bell's sinking is a sign that she is as sinful as the legendary nun, she attempts to reproduce the rest of the legend by flinging herself into the lake. Catherine sees sexuality as unmanageable and destructive. The community's idealization of her as nonpassionate can only add to her sense of passion's menace.

The danger of denying passion is also shown in Michael, who, like Catherine, has been in love with Nick. Michael has attempted to control his homosexuality by imposing religious conventions on himself but has succeeded only in disguising his feelings, even from himself. In *The Bell*, Murdoch treats homosexuality, like incest, as love for what is most like the self and implies that Michael must renounce it, but she also treats his refusal of the love that still exists as an immoral action. Her position is put into words by the Abbess: "all our failures are ultimately failures in love. Imperfect love must not be condemned and rejected, but made perfect." Michael briefly attempts this perfecting of love after he hears the old bell ringing, but he is easily deterred when Nick proves hostile. Murdoch attributes his failure to his feelings of guilt which, she implies, are masochistic and antagonistic to change. She thus makes intrapsychic the sadomasochism traditional to Gothic. Like the stance of the traditional Gothic heroine, Michael's position is fundamentally masochistic, and he substitutes suffering guilt for control of his faults.

The bell which calls Michael has been rung by Dora. Like James and Michael, Dora has submitted to conventions. She is "Dora, the cultivated woman" or "Mrs. Greenfield." Her resulting ignorance of her inner life is, like James's and Michael's, destructive, for combined with an equal ignorance of others, it results in a disastrous marriage. A potential for self-knowledge is indicated, however, in her occasional assertion of the self existing under all the roles. Further, despite her acceptance of patterns for herself, Dora refuses to force them on others: "a certain incapacity for 'placing' others stood her here in the lieu of virtue." She cannot see othes clearly, but at least she does not compound her ignorance by imposing false shapes upon them.

Dora's moral growth begins precisely because she refuses to accept the pattern Imber Court imposes on Catherine. Because they are both menaced by the community's denial of their reality, Dora identifies with Catherine and, inspired by her feelings about the girl, finally rejects the idea of herself the others hold. Yet, she has nothing to substitute for this idea because she has never learned who she really is. Because she does not feel like a real person in a real world, she has "the odd feeling that all this was inside her head. . . . It was as if her consciousness had eaten up its surroundings." She makes some contact with reality in the National Gallery, where art appears as an undeniably exterior reality, but, for Dora, art alone is not enough to prompt continuing virtue, and she soon feels again that Imber "would make her play their role." Thus, when she hears from Toby of his finding the old bell, she decides to use the bell for revenge on the community. The community has frustrated her attempt to reach out to the world, and the impulse which led her to it becomes diverted into a sadistic use of power.

Dora finally contacts reality through the old bell. The language used in the scene between Dora and the bell is curiously sexual: the bell was "mastering her and would have its will." She "stood beside it in the darkness, breathing hard. A thrill of terror and excitement went through her." The bell is associated with more than sexuality, however, for it is also encircled with pictures of the life of Christ which, Dora realizes, were "to the artist not an object of . . . imagination. These scenes had been more real to him than his own childhood." The old bell thus represents sexuality which has been directed to the outside world through the transforming powers of religion and art. In the presence of the bell, Dora regrets her misuse of power and recognizes that she is doing potential harm to the community. She is concerned about what she is doing to others. In other words, she loves. She uses the ringing of the bell to proclaim her actions and her recognition of reality.

Dora then achieves moral growth. Throughout the novel, however, the characters portrayed as most often channeling passion in realistic, loving ways are the nuns. The Abbess, for instance, is the only character who seems to guess a sexual relationship between Michael and Nick; yet she urges Michael to continue loving and associating with Nick. Mother Clare is at home in the bell's environment of the lake, can rescue Dora and Catherine from it, and is comfortable with her half-clothed body as she makes the rescue. The nuns also give a realistic atmosphere to the Abbey, symbolically suggesting transformation of Gothic impulses. When Toby, for instance, gazes across the lake at the Abbey and imagines the nuns walking "in meditation, their habits dragging on the grassy verge," they walk into view "at a brisk pace" with their skirts "hitched up a little to reveal stout black shoes." They are not meditating, but talking to one another, and one of them laughs "as clear as a bell," a laugh which fills Toby with "a sense of joy which seemed both physical and spiritual at the same time." In *The Bell*, the characters placed in the traditionally Gothic environment are thus most successful in growing into love.

In this affirmation of passion, there are, however, several notes of doubt. Passion, for instance, is affirmed in symbolic form only. Dora has contact with a bell, not a man, and the nuns are, after all, sworn to celibacy. Again, when Michael describes Dora's growth, he says she "fed like a glutton upon the catastrophes at Imber, and they had increased her substance." Surely his unpleasant comparison suggests that Dora's growth may actually come from incorporating the outer world, as she had once feared doing. Finally, doubt is revealed in Murdoch's treatment of Michael himself. Michael knows that he should avoid guilt; he knows that he should continue to love Nick; but he also knows that if he attempts to do so he will slip back into homosexuality. This is his assessment of himself, and, so far as the reader can tell, it is an accurate one. In creating Michael's dilemma, Murdoch places him in an impossible situation: she demands a love which is based on and includes passion but which the very strength of that passion makes impossible. In a sense, Murdoch confirms the danger of passion which the Imber Court residents already feel and which motivates them to deny it altogether. This fear of sexuality will come to prevail in *The Unicorn* and *The Time of the Angels*.

Unlike *The Bell*, *The Unicorn* (1963) is a full-fledged Gothic novel. Despite this submersion in Gothic, however, or indeed, because of it, the book portrays a smaller possibility for the transformation of sexual energy than does *The Bell*, for *The Unicorn's* total immersion in Gothic is a testimony to the overwhelming dangers and strengths of that world.

The Unicorn is set at Gaze Castle, in an isolated and ancient land, dotted with megaliths and dolmens. The pre-civilized quality of the setting makes it both a metaphor for and a fitting location for primitive sex and violence. The sea which pounds at the base of the Castle cliff, like the lake in *The Bell*, is connected with repressed impulses, and the thought of immersion in it produces in Marian, the governess, "a *frisson* which was like a kind of sexual thrill, both unpleasant and distressingly agreeable." Marian's mixed feelings toward the water are symbolic of her attitude toward sexuality: she is the traditional governess heroine, who simultaneously fears and desires passion.

The dangers and attractiveness of passion symbolized by the sea are also apparent in Gerald Scottow, whose overt and compelling sexuality makes him the traditional Gothic male. Gerald's sexual relationships, however, are homosexual or sadistic or both, indicating that like the Gothic villain-hero, he possesses untransformed passions. He is nonetheless irresistibly attractive to the others, particularly Marian, her employer Hannah, and Hannah's husband Peter and cousin Jamesie.

Marian experiences the result of passion by witnessing it in Hannah Crean-Smith, with whom she identifies, as is indicated by her wearing Hannah's clothing and assuming her punishment of confinement to Gaze (Morton Neil Kaplan, "Iris Murdoch and the Gothic Tradition," Diss. Columbia, 1969). As the novel opens, however, Hannah's sexuality is heavily repressed, and she leads a life of self-denial symbolized in classic manner by confinement in a house. Denis, one of Hannah's followers, compares her to a "nun," and neighbor Max Lejour explains the possibility for good in her passivity by using the concept of Até:

> Até is the name of the almost automatic transfer of suffering
> from one being to another. . . . Good is not exactly powerless.
> For . . . to be a complete victim, may be another source of power.
> But Good is non-powerful. . . . [A good person] only suffers and
> does not attempt to pass the suffering on.

Yet, the Gothic nun often represented hidden passion rather than holiness, and Murdoch implies that Hannah's self-denial becomes what Max calls "powerlessness," a means to control others. Hannah enjoys her role as a sufferer, and she demands that others share this fantasy with her. "I needed my audience," she says, looking back on herself. "I lived in your gaze like a false God." Hannah has lived in Gaze Castle and in the gaze of others; her decision to stay in the one is linked to her inability to live without the other. Murdoch elsewhere notes that sex "is connected with this sort of worshipping and extension of power, with the way in which we make other people play roles in our lives—dominating roles or slave roles." In the Gothic world of *The Unicorn*, Hannah's self-denial is actually masochism resembling the masochistic sexuality in which she has participated with Peter and in which she will participate with Gerald. Like Michael Meade, she remains passive so that a situation she enjoys can continue.

Hannah's followers, of course, cooperate in creating the myth of Hannah as pure sufferer. The love they claim to feel for her is actually self-love, for they see only the fantasy they have created from their own needs. Only when Hannah breaks from this role by sleeping with Gerald are the others forced to look truly at one another and at themselves. Because the characters can then recognize the existence of other people, they can love them and experience sexuality as encountering another, rather than as a masochistic submission to another. Because Effingham, for instance, sees Alice as "other," he desires her. Because Marian can "see" Denis "properly," she wants sex with him. In the break from seeing Hanna as all-pure, sexuality is transformed from a self-absorbed to an other-recognizing form.

Yet, in this novel, love ultimately fails. It fails for Effingham who remains self-centered and himself recognizes that he has, "through egoism, through being in some sense too small, too trivial to interest the powers of that world, escaped from evil. But he had not either been touched by good." Love fails for Marian when Hannah, who has been thrown over by Gerald, asks her to attempt living in genuine love at Gaze, and both are tempted back into the myth. Moreover, Marian and Denis are led back into the myth by the very sexuality which had seemed to recognize others. Denis returns to Hannah, Marian believes, because after his own relationship with her and Hannah's with Gerald, he must now "think of Hannah as a woman who might be possessed." By the same token, Marian stays at Gaze because she wants to be with Denis and because the experience of her own sexuality allows her to recognize the real, sexual Hannah, who needs her. Thus, the love which should have been liberating leads back again to solipsism.

Finally, love fails for Hannah herself. The genuine love she once felt for Pip Lejour would seem to be her only hope for nondestructive love. "You loved me once," Pip pleads. "Call up the remnant of that love. It is your only hope of life." Unfortunately Hannah has engaged in Max's Até: "I suffered too much for you," she tells Pip. "The suffering did not end in me. I thrust it back towards you in resentment." When Hannah rejects Pip, Gaze is returned to the power of masochistic Gothic fantasies, a situation symbolized by the now complete ascension to power of Gerald. As aggressive sexuality incarnate, Gerald is the necessary counterpart to the masochistic role; Hannah's inability to love leaves him in control. The only way she can keep from obliterating herself by masochistically submitting to Gerald is to reverse the situation and obliterate him. She thus shoots him with Pip's gun. She frees herself from the Castle, however, only to kill herself by a leap into the sea. Passion has proved too much for her. She cannot transform it; its release for her can only be destructive.

The *Time of the Angels* (1966), too, presents a totally Gothic vision in which potential for the transformation of passion has disappeared. The title of the book refers to this state: "Angels are the thoughts of God," says one of its characters. "Now he has dissolved into his thoughts, which are beyond our conception in their nature and their multiplicity and their power." God is but one of the forces outside the self whose demise has left humans at the mercy of frightening internal forces they formerly shaped. *The Time of the Angels* offers little hope for finding new means of transformation.

The exemplar of newly-released passion is the clergyman, Carel Fisher. Like Hannah, Carel shapes the lives and thoughts of most of the other characters. Indeed, his daughter Muriel sometimes feels that she and the others do not exist in an external world but rather are "all just the shadows of his thoughts." Carel contacts others through sadism. "Only in the infliction of pain," he says, "is the effect so contained in the cause as to convince of the existence of others." The other characters, of course, cooperate masochistically to give Carel his dominant role, because he meets their needs to escape responsibility for themselves. In Carel, one sees the increasing pessimism of Murdoch's Gothic novels, for the clerical figure in them has metamorphosized from *The Bell*'s idealized Abbess, to *The Unicorn*'s nun-like Hannah, to sadist Carel Fisher.

The Gothic isolation surrounding Carel symbolizes his lack of contact with the outer world. *The Time of the Angels* takes place in London, but, in the midst of the city, its setting is even more isolated than that of *The Unicorn*. Carel's house is in a huge bombed-out area, and throughout most of the novel it is further cut off by a fog that makes it seem to have "no exterior," but rather to have "absorbed all other space into its substance."

The spiritual isolation of the Rectory's inhabitants results in their literal inability to make contact with others; the people within the house have difficulty getting out and the people outside the house have difficulty getting in. Carel's servant Pattie, for instance, who has also been his mistress, longs to become a refugee camp worker, "but the thought was like a prisoner's dream. . . .," because she shares Carel's passion to the extent of losing her own identity in his. She feels "knitted to Carel by bonds so awful that it was frivolity even to call them love. She was Carel." She can break from him only when she learns that Carel is sleeping with Elizabeth and concludes that she cannot tolerate the "suffering" involved in seeing them together. This limit to her masochism, coupled with and perhaps prompted by a temporarily happy love for Eugene, the Rectory janitor, finally enables Pattie to go to the refugee camps and attempt to minister to the needs of others without "self-satisfaction." That this outward-reaching love is not shown in the novel itself indicates the difficulty Murdoch has in portraying the love she holds up as essential.

While Pattie knows she is imprisoned at the novel's opening, Muriel is only just becoming aware of her confinement. Like Pattie, she half enjoys being closed in: she is "excited" by the fog which "seemed to symbolize everything which at this time she feared," and her fear in the fog seems "more like love than fear." Her growing discomfort with life at the Rectory is prompted by a secretiveness in Elizabeth the cause of which she finally learns: Carel and Elizabeth are sleeping together, and Elizabeth is Carel's daughter.

Muriel discovers the former by peeking through a crack into Elizabeth's room and seeing them reflected in a mirror. Her action recalls Carel's description of philosophy catching a glimpse of the "truth" of existence "through some crack, some fissure in the surface . . ." In this Gothic world, the "truth" of existence is the reality and pervasiveness of forbidden passion. That Muriel glimpses this "truth" in a mirror suggests her own involvement in it. She is "guilty of seeing, of knowing" something not only about Carel and Elizabeth but about herself as well. Thus, upon seeing them, Muriel stands "immobile as a tower, rigid, full." That the imagery used of Muriel is the phallic imagery also used of Carel suggests that she shares the primitive sexuality he embodies. Like Pattie, Muriel turns to Eugene as an alternative to Carel, but she and Eugene fail to see one another apart from stereotypes they have imposed. She thus fails to love and fails to break from her father.

As Pattie and Muriel cannot get out of the Rectory, people outside the house cannot get in. Visitors are constantly knocking on the door and being turned away. At first, they seem to represent the "clean-cut rational world" which would be shocked by events at Carel's house. Yet, at least in the cases of Carel's brother Marcus and social worker Anthea Barlow, their difference from the Rectory inhabitants is largely illusion. Anthea, for instance, is the woman whom all three Fisher brothers loved and on whose account Carel

seduced Julian's wife and fathered Elizabeth; and as Carel has actually taken
Elizabeth to his bed, images of Elizabeth "followed Marcus to his bed and
hung above his sleep." The hidden passionate natures of both Anthea and
Marcus are traditional to the Gothic mode, which often portrays passion
beneath the façade of socialized behavior. This is why Pattie is unsure whether
it would be Carel or the outside world which would be destroyed if the
world ever gained access to his house. Contact with the passionate Carel
could as easily vanquish the everyday world as the everyday world could
destroy passion.

The force which Murdoch offers to counter destructive passion is, as
one might expect, love. Unfortunately, in the Gothic world of this novel,
love is possible only in childhood, when it is appropriately self-absorbed.
Muriel, for instance, recalls a time when there was "just herself and Carel
together" and sees that as their most loving time. Pattie, too, remembers
a love in infancy: "Her mother . . . once provided a sort of love, an animal
clutch, which the adolescent Pattie recalled with an uncomprehending,
wistful gratitude." Even Eugene, the most loving of the Rectory inhabitants,
has lived a relatively loveless adulthood after an idyllic childhood. His love
for his son, Leo, was easy and happy only in Leo's childhood and, since he
did not love his wife, Pattie is the only other person he has loved. All this
suggests that only primitive love is possible, and problems come when the
transition to adult sexuality must be made. Indeed, the suggestion is that
adult sexuality is impossible. There is, then, no source of redemptive love
in the self-absorbed world of the Rectory.

In *The Bell*, Murdoch implies that sexuality remains untransformed
because people refuse to acknowledge it. Thus, the Gothic moments in that
book often symbolize the intrusion of the sexual into everyday life, an
intrusion whose recognition can lead to love. *The Unicorn* and *The Time of
the Angels*, however, indicate a growing fear that, within the Gothic context,
sexuality can only be acknowledged in a self-absorbed, sadomasochistic form,
with the demands of the inner world denying the existence of the outer. As
she progresses from one Gothic novel to another, Murdoch's tone becomes
increasingly pessimistic and the implication becomes unavoidable that a
venture into the Gothic world means entrapment therein. She thus turns to
other fictional means for exploring love and sexuality. *The Nice and the Good*
has its uncanny moments, but in its predominately realistic world a man
and a woman actually fall in love and marry, each gratifying his own needs
and the other's. Not all of her subsequent novels are so optimistic as *The
Nice and the Good*, but Murdoch never again tries to use the Gothic version
of sexuality as an adult basis for love.

ELIZABETH DIPPLE

The Black Prince *and the* Figure *of Marsyas*

Art can rarely, but with authority, show how we learn from pain, swept by the violence of divine grace toward an unwilling wisdom, as described in the first chorus of the Agamemnon in words which somehow remind us of Plato, who remained (it appears) so scandalously indifferent to the merits of Aeschylus.

—IRIS MURDOCH, *The Fire and the Sun: Why Plato Banished the Artists*

Murdoch's novels at their best—and so great has her authority become since *The Nice and the Good* that each succeeding book manages this best to some degree—can locate this painful knowledge for us with an immediacy we cringe under. Her repeated claim is that tragedy is difficult to write (for her probably only Shakespeare and Aeschylus have succeeded) and nonexistent in the real world, where so much is governed by the dark comedy of causality put into motion by our misuse of ourselves, others, the world, art—the whole range of things our ego operates upon. If tragedy does not enlighten our lives, pain certainly does push the unwilling psyche forward, force it on to a better path—or a worse one. The unattainable quest for goodness constitutes the most important idea in Murdoch's art, a quest too obscure for human beings to see clearly, and about which we usualy deceive ourselves when we think we are on it. The pain of Murdoch's art aims to pull us out

From *Iris Murdoch: Work for the Spirit.* © 1982 by Elizabeth Dipple. Methuen & Co. Ltd., 1982. Originally entitled "Art and Theory."

of ourselves, just as her characters are pulled, so that something of the real good can be perceived.

The *locus classicus* of this phenomenon of pulling the self from the self is the Apollo-Marsyas myth, which has hung in the background of western art for centuries. Its connections to the moral-spiritual aspirations of mankind are strong and its application to our experience of life profound. In the myth Marsyas, a mortal of uncommon musical abilities, hubristically challenges the god of music Apollo to a contest, which Marsyas of course loses. His penalty is flaying—a horrible and painful death. In Ovid's version, he cries out in agony, "Quid me mihi detrahis?" (Why do you draw me out of myself?) According to Edgar Wind in *Pagan Mysteries in the Renaissance* (1968), to whom this paragraph is indebted, the Neoplatonists interpreted this pulling of the self from the self as a Bacchic pain leading to the clarity of Apollo, and Lorenzo de Medici declared that the way to perfection was by this road. The ordinary human who aspires to the transcendent is overwhelmed and shrieks with pain under the disproportionate strength of the god: to aim so high involves tearing off the earth to achieve the divine ecstasy. The longed-for confrontation with the god involves pain to the death, and the achievement of art surprises by the disproportion of this awful demand to our human, quotidian frame. The Christian centuries perceived the myth as a poetic theology, a perfect fusion of art and reality (the divine), and as such, Dante used the myth to open the first Canto of the *Paradiso*.

In *A Fairly Honourable Defeat*, Murdoch applies the Apollo-Marsyas myth to the homosexual couple, Simon and Axel, very briefly but powerfully. Simon as usual is in a state of love wrung by anxiety as he tries to make Axel promise to love him forever. Axel, who tries to live safely by limiting the lies he believes inherent in absolute statement, dodges the issue, saying that he has not the faintest idea whether he will. Simon's reference to the myth is frivolous at first:

"You're Apollo and I'm Marsyas. You'll end by flaying me."
   "That's an image of love, actually, Apollo and Marsyas."
   "How do you mean?"
   "The agony of Marsyas is the inevitable agony of the human soul in its desire to achieve God."
   "The things you know."
   "The things you failed to learn at the Courtauld."
   "I don't believe it though. Someone is flayed really. And there's only blood and pain and no love."
   "You think our planet is like that?"

"I think our planet is like that."

"No redeeming grace?"

"None at all."

"None, Simon?"

"Well, only this kind."

Axel's interpretation of the myth as "the inevitable agony of the human soul in its desire to achieve God" is historically correct but rather academic, and Simon's statement of the horrible reality—"blood and pain and no love"—takes it away from its too formal definition. The most interesting thing in their conversation is the usefulness of the myth and the commitment of the human spirit to both interpretations. Pain is in waiting for mortals, and whether it can be transformed by ecstasy or seen only blankly, as pain without redeeming grace, depends entirely on the psyche experiencing the flaying. One is reminded of Henry in *Henry and Cato* looking at Titian's *Death of Actaeon* and remarking that these goddesses are killers, and in *The Unicorn* Hannah Crean-Smith uses the image of the leaping salmon returning to their spawning pools in the same way, with the same idea of human bravery in entering another element: "It's a most moving sight. They spring right out of the water and struggle up the rocks. Such fantastic bravery, to enter another element like that. Like souls approaching God."

In Murdoch's working proof, however, the pain and bravery are not really thought out in advance by the participant, and the soul leaps as Marsyas did, with egotistic hubris and no grasp of the consequences or of the powerful side issues and apparently random elements which accompany any step forward to *exstasis* (a standing outside of, a result of separating the self from the self). The pain that drives one forward has not been bargained for, and is terrible and bitter. To this pain and death Murdoch's characters are frequently subjected, and, occasionally, through a forced knowledge of them, they achieve a partial redemption.

[Murdoch's] most extended use of the Marsyas myth and its consequences occurs . . . in what I consider her best novel so far, *The Black Prince* (1973). The last twenty-four pages of *The Fire and the Sun* set out firmly and eloquently Murdoch's view of the uses of art, and prove again even more powerfully than her well-reasoned earlier essays had done what an extraordinarily clear and radical theoretical literary critic she is. But *The Black Prince* embodies the doctrine she preaches and shows broadly and deeply the manifold operations of art in a particular man's use and pursuit of it. As a novel, it illustrates the profound and essential practice of irony, which Murdoch claims the artist must use and which is more natural in describing the real lives of human beings than the peculiar grand abstractions of tragedy. In recounting Plato's point of view in *The Fire and the Sun*, Murdoch tells us that he disallows the existence of the good artist, who in Murdoch's definition should "imitate the calm unenvious Demiurge who sees the re-calcitrant jumble of his material with just eyes, and with a commanding sense of proportion." What Plato does describe is the bad and mediocre artists, and Murdoch agrees with him. The bad artist is "a naive fantasist . . . and construes the world in accordance with the easy unresisted me-chanical "causality" of his personal dream life (the bad thriller or facile romance and its client)," and the mediocre artist

> thinks he "knows himself but too well," parades his mockery and spleen as a despairing dramatic rejection of any serious or just attempt to discern real order at all. This figure (a fairly familiar one in the pages of Plato's dialogue, where he is criti-cized, and of modern literature, where he is indulged) is on the road toward the "all is permitted" and "man is the measure of all things" of the cynical sophist. Neither of these, as artist or as man, possesses true self-knowledge or a just grasp of the hardness of the material which resists him, the necessity, the ἀνάγπη of the world. Confronted with semi-chaos the Demiurge is steadied (if he needs it) by the presence of the Forms. But must the mortal artist, condemned to some variety of self-in-dulgence, be either a dreamer or a cynic; and can he not attempt to see the created world in the pure light of the Forms?

In achieving good art and this view of Platonic reality, as Murdoch argues through the shifting progress of *The Black Prince*, the artist finds irony his most accurate tool. This is not the ironical self-flattering delusion of the mediocre artist, but irony induced by the duality of our experience, our highly developed sense of the comic on the one hand and the inevitable pain of our existence on the other, both exacerbated and driven often to absurdity by our obsessional prejudices and need to belittle others.

Irony is certainly the primary operative method in the framed, integ-umental structure of *The Black Prince*. The enclosure of a realist tale (which is simultaneously a love story, an adventure story and a dramatization of a theory of art) by an elaborate system of qualifying forewords and postscripts, as well as by intrusions into the narrative of what profess to be highly self-conscious truth-telling addresses to the editor, forces the reader into a world of multiple points of view. In this world where the human consciousness of the artist-protagonist strives towards clarity and just account, contradiction abounds and characters lose no opportunity to gainsay or diminish the most passionately expressed and convincing truths. The device of forewords and postscripts shatters the security of a highly-structured tale whose crafted design, even without these ironic addenda, is itself broken by intrusive apostrophes and the shifting nature of the narrative voice or persona. The pun on Pearson-person-persona is surely intentional. (Because Murdoch is obviously playing with Bradley Pearson's name, not only in this pun, but in the BP initials which equate him with the Black Prince of the title, I have decided to use the initials as an acronym in referring to him. I also suspect that the name Bradley may be intended playfully to evoke F. H. Bradley, the English idealist philosopher whose famous book, *Appearance and Reality*, was really a study of the Absolute. And of course the shadow of the Shakespearean critic, A. C. Bradley, casts its pall, as Richard Todd has pointed out in *Iris Murdoch: The Shakespearian Interest*, 1979.) The density of the tale constantly works against its clarity, and Bradley Pearson as both self-conscious artist and literary critic is at once achieving art and illustrating its pain and impossibility: Marsyas always loses, and yet the losing provides the *extasis*, the human achievement and the ultimate contact with divine "other" reality.

BP, as narrator and central character of *The Black Prince*, is both a good and bad aesthetician and moral thinker, constantly reflecting on the auto- biographical work of art he is in process of unravelling for us. In one of his elevated moments, his first direct address to his "dear friend" and great teacher—the editor whose identity is at first obscure to the reader—he discusses art's difficulty in finding a method of telling the truth. Both simplicity and complexity can be used, but because truth is so slippery and multiform and the human artist automatically limited by his own person- ality, irony exists both positively, as a just device in presenting our duality, and negatively, in our use of it to misuse others:

> Of course, as you have so often pointed out, we may attempt to attain truth through irony. (An angel might make of this a concise definition of the limits of human understanding.) Almost any tale of our doings is comic. We are bottomlessly comic to each other. Even the most adored and beloved person is comic to his lover. The novel is a comic form. Language is a comic form, and makes jokes in its sleep. God, if He existed, would laugh at His creation. Yet it is also the case that life is horrible, without metaphysical sense, wrecked by chance, pain and the close pros- pect of death. Out of this is born irony, our dangerous and necessary tool.
>
> Irony is a form of "tact" (witty word). It is our tactful sense

of proportion in the selection of forms for the embodying of beauty. Beauty is present when truth has found an apt form. It is impossible finally to separate these ideas. Yet there are points at which by a sort of momentary artificiality we can offer a diagnosis. . . . How can one describe a human being "justly"? How can one describe oneself? With what an air of false coy humility, with what an assumed confiding simplicity one sets about it. . . . How the angels must laugh and sigh. Yet what can one do but try to lodge one's vision somehow inside this layered stuff of ironic sensibility, which, if I were a fictitious character, would be that much deeper and denser? How prejudiced is this image of Arnold, how superficial this picture of Priscilla! Emotions cloud the view, and so far from isolating the particular, draw generality and even theory in their train.

Murdoch is quite aware of the further irony of her own falsely subjective method, since BP is indeed a character in a work of fiction whose book is about him and his friends. Murdoch's technique nevertheless brings off successfully an illustration of the problems involved in presenting the world as it is, in practising realism.

The Black Prince is a tale of the process of potential human development; its centre is the reality of the leap into another element as opposed to fantasizing or theorizing about it. The Marsyas who would create art is not praised and lionized as BP wishes to be, but metaphorically flayed, and his final, genuine relatedness to Apollo, the divine reality of good art, is gained only at this immeasurably painful price. Murdoch's decision to translate this mythic idea into fiction is extraordinarily adventuresome and very risky indeed, especially as it is necessarily woven into the fabric of her persistent moral and realist concerns. Not only must the artist have himself pulled from himself; all experience of the world and the whole of human moral life demand the same transformation. Hence the artist cannot be seen (as BP originally saw him) as a solitary chosen being separated from participation by the holiness of his gift, nor can he safely think that the dark creative Eros functions simply or will choose the route of his mere talent.

The naïve BP of the plot had believed in an easy and sacred-romantic definition of the artist. But as we begin reading this elaborate book, we come first to a peculiar Editor's Foreword by P. Loxias, who is anxious to give himself a vast role as BP's impresario, clown, harlequin and judge, and who reserves the last word for himself; we are thrust into an obscure world where a heavily disguised Apollo figure claims to be the *alter ego* of the writer of the love story we are now embarking upon. The identification probably has its source in Aeschylus, where in the *Agamemnon* Cassandra addresses her god Apollo as Loxias as she strips herself of her prophetic garment and prepares to die. We first meet the narrator, Bradley Pearson, after this editor has presented him and the novel to us. BP instantly explains his method of proceeding, saying he will "adopt the modern technique of narration, allowing the narrating consciousness to pass like a light along its series of present moments, aware of the past, unaware of what is to come." This past point of view is opposed to some new knowledge that he has achieved since the events of his story, some secret which is at the base of his new personality:

> The virtues have secret names: they are, so difficult of access, secret things. Everything that is worthy is secret. I will not attempt to describe or name that which I have learnt within the disciplined simplicity of my life as it has latterly been lived. I hope that I am a wiser and more charitable man now than I was then—I am certainly a happier man—and that the light of wisdom falling upon a fool can reveal, together with folly, the austere outline of truth.

Putting these things together produces no immediate sum for the reader, and although we know the authorial voice has a double persona— that of the past as opposed to the wiser one of the present—we are still in a considerable state of confusion as the one voice begins and the other intercepts. The primary voice, that of the artificial narrating persona of the past, is given to precious statements about the sanctity of the artist and his role as a saint who has "kept his gift pure" and reached "only a perceptive few":

> "A writer" is indeed the simplest and also the most accurate general description of me. In so far as I am also a psychologist, an amateur philosopher, a student of human affairs, I am so because these things are a part of being the kind of writer that I am. I have always been a seeker. And my seeking has taken the form of that attempt to tell the truth of which I have just spoken. I have, I hope and believe, kept my gift pure. This means, among other things, that I have never been a successful writer. I have never tried to please at the expense of truth. I have known, for long periods, the torture of life without self-expression. The most potent and sacred command which can be laid upon any artist is the command: wait. Art has its martyrs, not

least those who have preserved their silence. There are, I hazard, saints of art who have simply waited mutely all their lives rather than profane the purity of a single page with anything less than what is perfectly appropriate and beautiful, that is to say, with anything less than what is true.

This is obviously and irritatingly the kind of desperate, lying rationalization that characterizes failure, but when the other voice of the wiser present breaks in it yet retains some aesthetic view of art's separation from real life, and needs the modification of the Apollo figure who had claimed instantly that the tale to be presented is art in its truest form—a realistic description of human pain and transformation. This Apollonian truth makes Bradley's original and precious ideas about purity and silence simply frivolous:

Man's creative struggle, his search for wisdom and truth, is a love story. What follows is ambiguous and sometimes tortuously told. Man's searchings and his strugglings are ambiguous and vowed to hidden ways. Those who live by that dark light will understand. And yet: what can be simpler than a tale of love and more charming? That art gives charm to terrible things is perhaps its glory, perhaps its curse. Art is a doom. It has been the doom of Bradley Pearson. And in a quite different way it is my own.

The original BP persona, at the point where his "novel" begins, thought he was a servant of a real, vaguely supernal truth which demanded removal from life (i.e. London) to a seaside solitude uncontaminated by all too mortal and ordinary others, and perhaps demanded also a saintly martyrdom, should his attempt to create fail and he achieve only continued silence. He also perceives art as a talent which is his doom, but as he describes this doom he sounds precious rather than convincing, pretentious rather than genuinely truth-telling. The foreword of his Apollonian editor, reread after the novel has played out its elaborate structure, changes and gives a hard reality to a vocabulary that BP begins by using frivolously. If I may for clarity's sake speak of the unflayed (i.e. the pre-trial) BP as the primary narrating voice and the flayed (i.e. imprisoned with P. Loxias as teacher and companion) BP as the secondary voice, this Apollonian personification is aligned to the secondary voice, and like it can present words, terms, phrases with hard reality, whereas the naive primary voice misuses them out of ignorance and hubris.

It is the secondary, educated voice of BP who presents the novel (without forewords and postscripts) entitled *The Black Prince: A Celebration of Love*.

The blind and hubristic primary voice of BP is the basic narrator, however, and knows nothing at first of either celebration or love. From the first two prefatory pages we have the Apollo figure obscurely telling us what the process of the novel will finally bring home—a precise knowledge of what the hackneyed term "love story" means; not the romance of an elderly man, but "man's creative struggle . . . for wisdom and truth," which can be told only "ambiguously" and "tortuously," which is "secret," which is "a doom." These words are signals for our reading of the novel, and ways of talking about the density of human experience connected by a firm causality which emerges in this work of art devoted to presenting that experience as form.

That life is automatically opposed to form poses the first irony of the novel, an irony expressed by the need of both "author" and "editor" to tamper through prefatory and postscript material, to modify and extend the tight form of the finished art work itself, a product which Murdoch herself paradoxically speaks through and is invisible from. Just as Shakespeare projected the nervous and contradictory structure of *Hamlet* which will become so important in this work, Murdoch presents the Chinese box structure of this integumental and difficult novel. The story itself has a very pure form, and one that BP as an artist is anxious to retain. Scrupulously considering his structure on page one, he points out that there are from the beginning several ways of seeing the thing. Nervous about and inimical to conventional art forms, he explains that beginnings are entirely arbitrary. The "dramatically effective" one would use Arnold's phone-call stating that he thinks he has just killed his wife Rachel (with a poker), and end in neat circularity with Rachel's phone-call summoning BP as a witness to her having indeed killed her husband (with a poker). This neat structure would suggest that the story is the drama of Arnold Baffin's murder, which in a way it is. BP, however, chooses "a deeper pattern" of causality or consequence and begins with Francis Marloe's arrival to announce that BP's ex-wife Christian has returned to London from America. This return begins the long and complex action which leads BP to his murder trial, and focuses thus on him and hence "man's creative struggle" rather than on Arnold and Rachel. In other words, BP's self-consciously iterated choice means that the murder and revenge theme which makes this novel in a sense a general thriller is encapsulated by more serious concerns. The artist-narrator chooses so that structure can enlarge rather than reduce the subject matter.

As Murdoch presents BP in his primary voice he is an extremely precious, hellenistic perfectionist—a Rimbaud character filled with theories about art, and hence fussily enslaved to form, which he cannot produce. Given the right experiential circumstances, the early BP could, at best, force pen to paper and produce a neatly constructed, bloodlessly contrived adventure story, thriller, love story, tale of error and consequence. But in the terms controlled by the Niagara force of the present narrative, the fastidious BP is rendered, at one level, in simple and gross terms as a naïve and barren follower of Rimbaud who can be seen as plunged into the loosening experience of a love adventure which, as his own postscript warns, can be simplistically interpreted as driving away his writer's block and forcing him to write, at another level entirely new to him, a good, racy, autobiographical quasi-work of art. But this novel is preeminently about transformation and metamorphosis, and we must therefore from the beginning deal with the secondary, transformed, educated voice who, together with the Loxias figure, conspires against form and undercuts it wherever possible.

The paradoxical conjunction of form and formlessness is very important in Murdoch's thinking about art. She described it in an interview with Michael Bellamy (1977) as the "conflict between the form-maker and the truthful formless figure," and certainly it is the basis of the contrast in her work between the would-be artist and the would-be saint, even perhaps in such a novel as *A Fairly Honourable Defeat* between evil and good, as the struggle of Tallis versus Julius will illustrate. In BP Murdoch has constructed a character who, after his education, combines qualities of both and shows through his experience the subtle linking of art and ethics when they perform their proper truth-telling function.

The primary artist BP forms the artwork, while the secondary, ethical, experienced, clear-sighted BP tampers and interrupts, destroying the neatness of the form by deliberately interjecting a contradictory impulse toward disunity. This antiformal impulse, however, is exactly the factor that removes BP's novel from the domain of the mediocre, and because of it a vulgar estimation of the book as merely the story of an elderly man in love with a young girl or of a violent murder is entirely incorrect. Not only is Murdoch fusing the artist with the ethical thinker, but she is showing also how the painful winning of knowledge and in some measure a perception of reality enlarge the scope and texture of art. The secondary voice frequently breaks the form, as does Apollo-Loxias himself in his forewords and postscripts, because formlessness delivers truth even while it here coexists at first so confusingly and finally so fruitfully with form.

Although the primary BP tries to depict himself and his feelings at the pre-educational time of the action, the secondary voice several times interrupts the "story" to address his dear friend in a "direct speaking," a device the two have discussed and decided is legitimate. These interruptions are devoted to ruminations on the function and nature of art, as well as of its task in the human struggle towards reality:

> Art . . . is the telling of truth, and is the only available method for the telling of certain truths. Yet how almost impossibly difficult it is not to let the marvels of the instrument itself interfere with the task to which it is dedicated.

One of the functions of these interruptions is to restrain the slickness of the instrument or form, to slow down and deepen a plot which is whirling quickly by, and above all to concentrate on "the task to which it is dedicated." "My book is about art," BP has said immediately before this quotation, and since a definition and description of art constitute the task at hand, it is crucial that we discern the process and instruments of that definition.

The Black Prince is Murdoch's fictional manifesto, her pouring into fiction of her best thinking about art itself and its relationship to human behaviour and development. The process of defining resides in the progress of the novel, and by hanging the plot on the character of BP she allows his journey from ignorance to knowledge to become the image of her definition. The task of the reader is to perceive the Pearson persona clearly, to know what BP understands at any given point, to estimate justly. The complexities imposed on the plot by interruptions and denials of unity in structure or point of view are part of the unfolding and hold the reader when the irritating and flawed primary BP in his confusion wanders wide of our sympathy. Above all, the fact of a plot gives Murdoch the basic material for her central claim that experience is better than the "demons of abstraction," and that art and morality are interwoven in substance: "all art is the struggle to be, in a particular way, virtuous."

Implicit throughout this novel is a demand that this state of equivalence between art and morality be recognized. Just as Dora in *The Bell* underestimated the medieval bell, perceiving it inadequately and applying it destructively to her own ego, the primary voice of BP and the four writers of the postscripts who fail to engage in a just and moral estimation of his story are involved in a double failure: a failure to recognize the truth of the art object and a failure to make an adequate moral judgement. Although Murdoch's subject is the description and definition of art, one important corollary is thoroughly examined: the nature of literary criticism and the responsibility of the critic. In this Murdoch is very unfashionable, for, as she argues in *The Fire and the Sun*, "learning to detect the false in art and enjoy the true is part of a lifelong education in moral discernment," and *The Black Prince* shows the result of the lack of such discernment. Bad criticism, rendered inaccurate through the ego-interference of the critic, is severely attacked in this novel, and the contempt of Loxias for the self-serving postscript writers can also be directed against all critics whose cowardice and failure in moral engagement cause them to belittle the object.

In *The Fire and the Sun*, Murdoch says that "the final best instrument" in criticism is "the calm open judging mind of the intelligent experienced critic, unmisted, as far as possible, by theory." The primary voice of BP is not only misted but clogged with theory, some of it good, most of it bad. The theories he holds refer to his own artistic career and offer consolation for his purity and meagre output; they also give him ample material for attacking Arnold Baffin, with whom he quarrels manically and compulsively on the subject at every chance. The fairly long excerpt BP quotes of his review of Arnold's new book typifies bad, self-serving, theory-ridden criticism, a criticism which reflects on itself (and the critic's self) rather than on the object at hand. The reader has really no doubt (given the plot summary of it) that Arnolds's book is bad, but naïve Julian is the better and more reliable critic when she comically addresses her father's work directly and objectively: "He lives in a sort of rosy haze with Jesus and Mary and Buddha and Shiva and the Fisher King all chasing round and round dressed up as people in Chelsea."

Murdoch is of course using Arnold's prolificacy and BP's contempt of it as an ironic echo of the journalistic attacks she herself has received. A self-critical writer constantly refining her style, Murdoch heself could be speaking Arnold's words:

> You, and you aren't the only one, every critic tends to do this, speak as if you were addressing a person of invincible complacency, you speak as if the artist had never realized his faults at all. In fact most artists understand their own weaknesses far better than the critics do. Only naturally there is no place for the public parade of this knowledge. If one is prepared to publish a work one must let it speak for itself. It would be unthinkable to run along beside it whispering "I know it's no good." One keeps one's mouth shut.

Tongue in cheek, she presents Arnold possibly as a parody of Anthony Powell, but also of what some critics have accused her of being because of her mysterious allusive frame and awesome prolificacy. In BP's self-justifying attacks on Arnold, however, Murdoch is exploring a serious failure of insight and moral discrimination, a failure of calmness which inhibits the development of the coolly judging mind and leads to a violent act of jealousy when BP rips up in ten wild minutes every volume of Arnold's entire huge *oeuvre*. This symbolic murder of Arnold is a foreshadowing in the world of art of what Rachel performs in the world of experience. BP's trial, as he himself feels, is partly an exorcism of a very real guilt.

He manages good criticism only when his transformation has begun and he is talking about *Hamlet* to Julian, immediately before recognizing that he is in love with her. In his extraordinary monologue on the peculiar nature of Shakespeare's achievement in projecting both experienced feeling and spiritual energy into the play, BP suddenly transcends his typical jealous grumbling and perceives a work of art radically and originally. His eloquent insight allows a fusion of the various elements in his usual vocabulary about art and the artist, and this central moment with its dense, allusive perception articulates many of the issues about the role of the artist which, up to this point in the novel, have been so puzzling. This is, in short, good criticism, because BP is concentrating his considerable intelligence and originality on something outside himself, on an artist so good that his own mean-spirited competitiveness and personal neuroses are simply swept away.

The most important point about this eloquence in the midst of the novel's fast, almost Dionysian process is that it is prompted by the rapid approach of a metamorphosis in BP's character and life prompted by, indeed entirely coinciding with, his falling in love with young Julian. In the progress of BP's adventures, he had previously shown an inclination to believe that perhaps the sudden, unnerving crowding-in of experience that he had been undergoing, and particularly the growing affair with Rachel Baffin, Julian's mother, might be instrumental in his writing his great book. "Was I upon the brink of some balls-up of catastrophic dimensions, some real disaster? Or was this perhaps in an unexpected form the opening itself of my long-awaited 'break through,' my passage into the presence of the god?" That the two—disaster and contact with the god—might coincide did not occur to him, but he had perceived that a metamorphosis associated with personal destiny and somehow controlled by a divine power was in store for him:

> And yet, so complex are minds and so deeply intermingled are their faculties that one kind of change often images or prefigures another of, as it seems, a quite different sort. One perceives a subterranean current, one feels the grip of destiny, striking coincidences occur and the world is full of signs: such things are

> not necessarily senseless or symptoms of incipient paranoia. They
> can indeed be the shadows of a real and not yet apprehended
> metamorphosis. Coming events do cast shadows.

Instantly on perceiving that he incongruously but absolutely loves Julian,
he assumes that this is the final step, the real metamorphosis, and that the
affair's breakup will constitute the disaster. Only by extended painful as-
tonishment is he pulled beyond anything he had imagined, and with real
amazement the reader learns much later in the conclusion of the basic plot
and in the Editor's Postscript that the real end is death—Arnold's and, more
significantly in terms of this book's study of the nature of the artist, BP's
own.

The complex aesthetic ideology of the novel must be absorbed step by
step as Murdoch, her Apollo impresario and the two voices of BP present
it. Let us begin by looking at BP and his vocabulary. The primary voice—
the BP undergoing the experiences that lead to knowledge—is one of Murdoch's most highly-polished comic figures. For all the grimness of the secondary persona's cogitations, he steadily reasserts that human beings are
endlessly comic to each other. Defining what comedy is and how it can be
played out in the middle of action which can also be seen as full of pain
and horror is one of the many tasks of this novel.

The BP of the process of the book enacts a grim comedy at every turn
because the person he then was, as his knowledgeable later persona puts it,
was "captive and blind." The failure to coalesce intelligence and real perception, to see himself and his relations with those about him clearly, to
distinguish between his compulsive neuroses and the real state of things,
all contribute to the long process of enlightenment necessary. We have
therefore a character who, despite his carefully attained cultural expertise,
his sophistication, his narrow but real ability as a writer, his years of experience in the routine of the tax office, and his fifty-eight years of complex
human relationships, can be thrown easily into situation after situation in
which his neurotic compulsions rule and his actions comically fail to coincide
with the self-knowledge he wrongly believes himself to have. Captive to his
neuroses and mesmerized by a false image of himself, he is badly in need
of metamorphosis, of a pulling of the self from the self so that he can reach
the divine end in which he sees art (and Murdoch sees life) as participating.
But the comic genius of his presentation consists in the risible contrast
between the wisdom he believes he has and the tyranny of his compulsions.
It is clear from the novel that Murdoch sees this gap as the central idea of
comedy and, embellished by a wit which serves to heighten the distance

between personal ideas of the self and its reality, the novel only slowly unfolds the horror that the comedic circumstance leads to. "How the angels must laugh and sigh," as the secondary BP puts it. For Murdoch, comedy is a servant to seriousness and a necessary part of mimetic descriptions of real people.

BP's comic-tragic drama opens with a situation which is realistic, unfunny and rather dull. Its swirling into comedy and the speed of its causality occur against his will: he himself persistently believes that he is all ready to perform the great act of his life in writing a good book. Recently retired from years of tedium in the tax office in order to write, BP finds himself with an unexpected writer's block and decides to try for privacy and silence at a secretly rented cottage by the sea. Already packed and ready to leave, he fussily decides to check if he has packed his sleeping pills, his belladonna, his proper notebooks. This delaying tactic obviously reflects an unconscious knowledge that he is not at all ready and does not want to be in silence with himself, and in fact the unpacking completely smashes his plans for retreat. By casual chance, he is swept out of dullness into hectic action as Murdoch, in one of her typically manoeuvred *coups*, coalesces three crises in the lives of her main characters. Had BP not been nervous over his retreat, he would have escaped this dramatic juncture, but suddenly Francis Marloe descends on him to announce that Bradley's long-divorced wife Christian is back after her American marriage, Arnold phones to say he thinks he has murdered Rachel, and BP's sister Priscilla arrives on his doorstep to announce that she has left her husband and must be looked after. Each of these crises is played out to its irreversible end, all three intermingling with each other and all clawing at BP, who does in fact try to escape by turning to Julian, who at first had looked like only a side issue.

The speed of the action and BP's reaction to everyone and everything that swims into his ken constitute the novel's plot. The authorial control that causes the multiple crises of the other characters is perceived by BP as somehow connected to some cosmic intention. (This plot control can indeed be seen as reflective of the random condition of the universe: the issue is an interesting one in that those who wish to claim—and I do not—that Murdoch's plots are mere contrivances would deny that she could, in creating such circumstances, be in any way reflecting odd occurrences and concurrences in any human life.) As the plot overthickens, a frantic BP feels that he must get out of London or "something would reach out and grab me." His whole frame of reference centres on psychic projections of gods and powers whose metaphorical images serve as definitions of the ideas that obsess him. Until he is reluctantly caught up in the affairs of others and his relations

with them (he is caught up *because* of his relations with them, but he fails
to see this) these metaphorical ideas concern the abstract nature of great art
and his potentiality in producing it. Murdoch, however, believes with Plato
that truth must live in present consciousness, and for her this consciousness
is related not to abstract theories but to the details of the necessary moment.
BP is, therefore, generally wrong in his theories, but his vocabulary, as he
will later find out, may be occasionally correct, although wrongly understood. The experience from which he so ardently wishes to escape is the
necessary tool for purifying his knowledge of what art is.

In an earlier novel, *Bruno's Dream* (1969), Murdoch presents a pretype
of BP, Miles Greensleave, who is also an avoider of life's intensities and
whose talent and vocabulary are reminiscent of the early BP's. Both men
are essentially seen as silly as they work preciously and long on the purifying
of their talent; both are incapable of production. Miles spends endless hours
with his commonplace book, describing the delicacy of a flower or a wet
leaf on the windowpane; BP writes and writes his way through notebooks
to no avail. When BP speaks of his recognition of himself as an artist, he
speaks, with Miles's sort of self-aggrandizement, of a radiant experience of
seeing a fox: "the child wept and knew himself an artist." Like BP, Miles
has an egotistical conviction, not sustained by achievement, that his personality is conducive to the production of art, which he, too, refers to as
the visitation of a god. And like BP, Miles is jogged through the experience
of pain and deprivation into writing. But Miles is in all respects such a
negative character, and the nature of his final turning to poetry so unexplored,
that the reader is not at all convinced of his competence. The point that
this earlier character contributes to, however, is the tendency in Murdoch's
fictions about art to depict the artist as initially flawed and egocentric—and
as waiting for a god.

The whole metaphor is, of course, very Greek. It suggests the relationship of Apollo and the Muses and opens the way for our identification
of the Loxias figure. (It is significant that Arnold, the professional and popular
writer, claims to have no muse.) As the primary voice of BP sees it, however,
the external other which joins itself to the talented creator, the god whom
BP and Miles await, is the mythic Eros of the *Symposium* and *Phaedrus*. BP
interprets this figure narrowly as a certain kind of creative energy, and hence
as the power controlling the idea of art and its production. He feels obscurely
that at the right moment for composition he will be profoundly shaken by
this god, and he knows that "[his] development as an artist was [his]
development as a man." Yet his desperate need for silence and detachment,
his urge to get out of London and his repugnance at the messy involvements

he finds himself in the middle of all indicate that he misunderstands the nature of his relationship to this external god who rules not only the creation of art, but also the erotic centre of all human beings.

Murdoch, who argues so firmly for "strong agile realism," sees BP's fastidious recoil from the necessary present as an illustration of his inadequacy and blindness. Plunged into the untidy, generally depressing middle-aged erotic affairs of others—Rachel's and Arnold's violence, Priscilla's sad protracted failures, Francis Marloe's pitiable failed homosexuality, Christian's sleek flirtations, Roger and Marigold's uneven and cruel match—BP cannot perceive that these are where the real Eros resides. Self-consumed, he identifies this tumult with some alien power destructive of his creativity and becomes increasingly frantic to escape into solitude. It is only after he has been well taught through the process of the tale that he recognizes that the symbolic Eros extends his activity not mythically and abstractly, but in the real world with these messy characters whom BP must suffer and learn from. The compulsive, Dionysian speed of the action and of BP's mode of narrating it produce the present work of art—a work utterly unlike anything the primary fastidious persona of BP could have envisioned. Finally Apollo teaches Dionysian energy, but his major lesson is that the lived details of the present moment give the artist his material.

BP is wrong not only about the nature of artistic inspiration and what is required of the artist in terms of participation and observations but also about the composition of his own erotic self. His youthful divorce from Christian was followed by some affairs which he declines to talk about, and certainly Francis is partially right in his postscript when he says that BP's relationship to Arnold has homoerotic elements. Comically obsessed by the phallic Post Office Tower, he takes unanalysed steps to resume the connection with Christian, and becomes really interested in his now crazily complex milieu only when Rachel makes sexual overtures to him. Suddenly he remembers that his dark, veiled god, Eros, is sexual in most manifestations, and adds the image of Aphrodite to his arsenal of symbols. It occurs to him that "Rachel might indeed be the messenger of the god." Having an affair with her would take a new sort of courage: "It had often, when I thought most profoundly about it, occurred to me that *I was a bad artist because I was a coward.* Would now courage in life prefigure and even perhaps induce courage in art?" This dawning realization of art's dependence on life certainly is a first step forward for BP, and one that is both easy and pleasant: having an affair with Rachel which she will look after and keep from getting awkward would not significantly interfere with what he images as a visitation of Eros. His impotence when he actually finds himself in bed with her comically announces his failure in both areas of eroticism, and it is clear that he is far from ready for the creation of art. The secondary voice, in commenting on BP's muddle and inadequacy with Rachel (and with Priscilla, Francis, Arnold, Christian, *et al.*) indicates how removed that past self had been from any kind of insight:

> There is so much grit in the bottom of the container, almost all
> our natural preoccupations are low ones, and in most cases the
> rag-bag of consciousness is only unified by the experience of great
> art or of intense love. Neither of these was relevant to my messy
> and absentminded goings-on.

Still BP continues, as he enacts his tale, to feel that the new frenetic pace of his life is connected to the "hand of destiny," a destiny divided between a negative sense that some power is causing all this muddle and is out to get him and his positive belief that the visitation of the creative Eros ("a great dark wonderful something,") is imminent. So convinced is he that he can protect his ego from suffering and keep some kind of power over things that he is utterly taken by surprise when the process begins and he suddenly experiences an intense love which sets him on the path towards real art. Having fooled around with Rachel, BP now falls absolutely in love with young Julian, who has been unimpressively in the background from the beginning, ripping up love letters, childishly asking for BP's little bronze water buffalo lady, demanding that he tutor her, flying a balloon which he chases. After tumbling ignominiously out of bed with Rachel, he had stumbled into Julian and bought her an erection-producing pair of purple boots. So untuned to his erotic being is BP that none of these incidents registers, and it is only after Julian irritatingly appears to study *Hamlet* with him and he launches into the impassioned lecture-interpretation of Shakespeare's relationship to his masterpiece that he recognizes himself to be in the grip of a power he has no preparation for.

Falling in love with Julian affects BP in two ways. First he loves her as a real woman in the real world, and in this respect he acknowledges the inappropriateness of the situation. This novel is constructed carefully so that mirrored actions occur frequently, and here the January–May affair which earlier he had so brutally attacked in Roger and Marigold becomes his own dilemma. And just as he sees falling in love with Julian as a moment of revolution in his art, he receives a letter (the fatal letter which leads Rachel to murder her husband) from Arnold saying that he too has fallen in love, with Christian, and that this event will create a revolution in his art. These ironic doublings and repetitions help the novel's strong sense of the erratic and impenetrable, and therefore unjudgeable, nature of the world. Nevertheless, the sexual, erotic love for Julian is real, and BP experiences what he calls "a sort of incarnate history of human love." Certainly Murdoch's masterly eloquence through BP in describing the nature of being in love day by day is one of the most penetrating and exciting achievements of the novel.

But what is even more interesting in a theoretical way is the second level of BP's love for Julian. Here Murdoch shapes her central symbols into a tight coalescence which allows a subtle enactment of Eros's many creative energies. Julian's presence forces BP to think hard about *Hamlet* and Shakespeare, and his as yet unrecognized sexual response to her drives him to the intense and radical reevaluation he makes of that play. This erotic energy is then suddenly and fiercely focused on Julian, when she identifies herself with the artwork by saying, "I played Hamlet once." BP instantly feels that "she had filled me with a previously unimaginable power which I knew that I would and could use in my art." He feels that he has "become some sort of god" and at the same time recognizes the primary issue: "There was an overwhelming sense of reality, of being at last real and seeing the real. The tables, the chairs, the sherry glasses, the curls on the rug, the dust: real." Included in this complex experience is an evocation of the god. As BP renders Hamlet, he refers to the Marsyas-Apollo myth by identifying Hamlet with speech: "He is the tormented empty sinful consciousness of man seared by the bright light of art, the god's flayed victim dancing the dance of creation." Shakespeare in writing *Hamlet* is

> speaking as few artists can speak, in the first person and yet at the pinnacle of artifice. How veiled that deity, how dangerous to approach, how almost impossible with impunity to address, Shakespeare knew better than any man. . . . But because his god is a real god and not an *eidolon* of private fantasy, and because love has here invented language as if for the first time, he can change pain into poetry and orgasms into pure thought—.

Shakespeare's real god is not merely Eros but Apollo, and for the first time BP understands the pain Shakespeare through Hamlet is speaking about, the flaying, metamorphosis and wild energy of the whole enterprise. He knows that Shakespeare's god is a "real god and not an *eidolon* of private fantasy" as his own version of the dark Eros has been. Oddly enough, much of what BP says appears to come from his subconscious and not to be wholly retained. He does not replace the image of Eros with that of Apollo (and beyond) until his trial and education, after which he returns to this central insight: "And the black Eros whom I loved and feared was but an insubstantial shadow of a greater and more terrible godhead."

Nevertheless knowing at least some reality and anticipating pain take BP very far forward. Later, also in his postscript, he will describe Julian not as an end but as his gateway: "Human love is the gateway to all knowledge, as Plato understood. And through the door that Julian opened my being passed into another world." During the process of his love affair with her, however, his knowledge continues to be imperfect. The pain he inadequately envisages is first his own silence (which, as Francis points out, he breaks almost immediately), then the impracticality of the whole thing because of the age difference, then Arnold's fury and Rachel's burning jealousy and anger. He is completely unprophetic about the real results and still blind to the subtleties of causality: another large leap into the appalling unknown will be demanded.

The passage in which he envisions the confluence of all major elements enacts the life and intention of Murdoch's title: *Hamlet* points to Shakespeare, Hamlet to Julian, and all three to BP and Apollo and the creative Eros. Who, indeed, many readers have asked, is the Black Prince? Obviously and traditionally Hamlet, of course. But also Julian, who in dressing up as Hamlet enacts in flesh the Eros of BP's apprehension of art. Julian as Hamlet is what BP loves. (He is impotent in bed with her as he had been with Rachel until she costumes herself as the literary black prince. Through this prodding, BP's remembrance of Hamlet's pain gives substance—and violence—to his own horror at Priscilla's death, and rape results.) But there can be little doubt that the black Eros as dark god so often addressed must be considered the real black prince: the subtitle, *A Celebration of Love*, gives the clue to the mythological identity. There is more to come, however, and Francis Marloe in his not altogether mad postscript also rightly points out that BP's initials give him the right to the title. Finally there is Loxias-Apollo himself, whom BP will in conclusion address as "the crown of my quest":

> I was seeking you, I was seeking him, and the knowledge beyond
> all persons which has no name at all. So I sought you long and
> in sorrow, and in the end you consoled me for lifelong deprivation
> of you by suffering with me. And the suffering became joy.

What are we to do with all of these identifications of the title? "My book is about art," BP told us at the beginning of the novel, and P. Loxias had said that "Man's creative struggle, his search for wisdom and truth, is a love story." Eros as love at its highest, but including even its lowest reaches, commands the title, but the others participate in that title, as art at its most intense and serious toils to project an adequate definition. *Hamlet*, mythology, an ordinary girl, human brutality and vengeance, a talented but spiritually blinded man, all combine to define the erotic connecting energy between art and love and their power to point still further, beyond themselves.

Like BP, the reader could at this point falter, forgetting that Julian is only the gateway to the other world that BP enters. This qualification in no way diminishes her importance, and indeed BP links his capacity to write with her, using her as poets immemorially have done with their loves, celebrating her and conferring immortality on her: "She somehow was and is the book, the story of herself. This is her deification and incidentally her immortality. It is my gift to her and my final possession of her. From this embrace she can never now escape." BP's loss of Julian through his own subterfuge (not telling her instantly about Priscilla's death or the quasi-affair with Rachel) and lying (he says he is only forty-six), drives him backwards again to distraction and fantasy, but it is not at all the flaying of the Marsyas artist by the real god. BP much later points out that "the false god punishes, the true god slays." Julian's flight from him and her disappearance impose punishment, but he is in for much more.

The causality of BP's punishment in losing Julian is part of the larger pattern of inexorable cause and effect which governs this book. Given Murdoch's spiritual inclination towards the infinite and veiled idea of the good, it is natural that she uses it to fight against human failure by evoking it in relationship to causality: "The wicked regard time as discontinuous, the wicked dull their sense of natural causality. The good feel being as a total dense mesh of tiny interconnections. My lightest whim can affect the whole future." BP's secondary voice recognizes and comments on these tiny interconnections throughout. He also opposes form or art to the good, thus remaining within Murdoch's paradox of celebrating art and yet fighting it:

> One of the many respects, dear friend, in which life is unlike art is this: characters in art can have unassailable dignity, whereas characters in life have none. Yet of course life, in this respect as in others, pathetically and continually aspires to the conditions of art. A sheer concern for one's dignity, a sense of form, a sense of style, inspires more of our baser actions than any conventional analysis of possible sins is likely to bring to light. A good man often appears *gauche* simply because he does not take advantage

of the myriad mean little chances of making himself look stylish. Preferring truth to form, he is not constantly at work upon the facade of his appearance.

Although art may admire, it cannot easily proclaim the good, which is too undramatic and unglamorous. Plots of fascinating but devastating causality such as this one are produced by the activities of the infinitely punishable, guilty, average person:

> The natural tendency of the human soul is towards the protection of the ego. The Niagara-force of this tendency can be readily recognized by introspection, and its results are everywhere on public show. We desire to be richer, handsomer, cleverer, stronger, more adored and more apparently good than anyone else. I say "apparently" because the average man while he covets real wealth, normally covets only apparent good. The burden of genuine goodness is instinctively appreciated as intolerable, and a desire for it would put out of focus the other and ordinary wishes by which one lives. Of course very occasionally and for an instant even the worst of men may wish for goodness. Anyone who is an artist can feel its magnetism. I use the word "good" here as a veil. What it veils can be known, but not further named.

The main characters who act the plot through to its end—Bradley Pearson, Arnold and Rachel Baffin—are average people who do not particularly think about the good and indeed would find its blank face intolerable. Although their egos lead them to evil deeds, their intentions are no more than merely muddled.

It is extremely interesting that of all the characters, only the secondary, educated persona of BP in his "monastery" prison ponders what good might be, and in his wide-ranging use of religious vocabulary, connects it with sainthood. Wretched Francis Marloe comes closer than the other characters to fumbling thought on the subject as he tries incompetently to show his love for all others, but BP's ruminations are central and comprise Murdoch's device to illustrate how far, through his experiences and education, he has travelled. In the first place, he knows what a saint would be like and that, as Loxias has told him, none exists because the absolute relationship to the good implied imposes an intolerable burden on the personality: "A saint would identify himself with everything. Only there are, so my wise friend tells me, no saints." He also knows the right (or real) questions and their ultimate unanswerability: "What is it to love God?"; "What does the artist fear?"; "How can one change the quality of consciousness?"; "Can there be a *natural*, as it were Shakespearean felicity in the moral life? Or are the Eastern sages right to set as their task in their disciples the gradual total destruction of the dreaming ego?"; "Could constant prayer avail?"; etc.

A barren complete listing of these questions would fail to convey their contextual strength, and the strong sense Murdoch manages to get across is that reaching the questions belongs not to the quotidian but to another "world" or state of advancement into which BP has finally passed. But for all the emphasis on his passage, the quotidian or ordinary world is not forgotten, and Murdoch throughout the novel keeps it in focus with strong image patterns ranging from the absurdly funny (the phallic Post Office Tower, the mad recurrence of milk chocolate) to the very serious amulets which attach themselves to personality as possessive love objects (the water buffalo lady bronze, the snuff box inscribed "A Friend's Gift," statues of Aphrodite). In one most beautiful nexus of symbols from the real world, Murdoch evokes drifting, airborne objects—a balloon, kites, faces as radiant moons, huge pale globes, pigeons (being shot down)—and in talking of the kites, gives a touching description of part of their imagistic power: "What an image of our condition, the distant high thing, the sensitive pull, the feel of the cord, its invisibility, its length, the fear of loss."

Meanwhile, BP's love for Julian, his "gateway," imposes an interim metamorphosis on him. Like Marsyas, he enters the game blindly and perhaps hubristically, but it takes only a few days for him to realize how desperate his situation is, how inevitable his failures will be, and how in his "chess game with the dark lord" he may make "perhaps a fatally wrong move." Nevertheless, although consciousness may be unified (as BP tells us on p. 155) only "by the experience of great art or of intense love," this love requires a mode of description, and the one chosen is, typically enough, that of religion. This is partly because BP's whole story has a religious idea as its end, but more because in contemporary western experience religion is seen as a source of metaphor rather than as a lived belief. As M. H. Abrams pointed out in *Natural Supernaturalism* (1971), this secularization of inherited theological ideas and ways of thinking dates from the great romantics, and it is in a way artistically natural that BP's transformation be given particularity and intensity when a religious mode of discourse once central to our culture is enlisted to its aid. Filled with his still secret love for Julian, BP talks to Christian (the women's names are not accidental), who sees him thus: "Brad, what is it, you look extraordinary, something's happened to you, you're beautiful, you look like a saint or something, you look like some goddam picture, you look all young again." And later, she describes him again as a saint and identifies the change with Christ's mystical temporary transfiguration. Julian's name, as usual in Murdoch's many evocations of the saint of Norwich, gains even more pointed significance as BP associates her with the famous words, "All shall be well and all shall be well." He returns to his flat, now made divine by her visit to it: "So holy men return to temples and crusading knights feed upon the blest sacrament."

The love affair takes a firm step forward, comically in the restaurant on the Post Office Tower, seriously through the intensity of art, as BP and Julian attend a performance of Richard Strauss's *Der Rosenkavalier* at Covent Garden. Here BP, who previously disliked music and was irritated by Arnold's passion for it, is pushed by Julian's presence not merely to listen to the soaring opening duet, but to "undergo it." The focusing caused by love's interaction with art here, as in the lecture on *Hamlet*, leads to a crisis, as this fastidious man rushes from the intensity of the music and vomits violently. His vomiting involves an acknowledgement of his body, of the messiness of human physical being, which BP has hitherto associated only with Rachel and the vomiting and suicidal Priscilla. This reminder of himself allows his confession to Julian and the launching of their affair. Pursued by Arnold's outrage and Rachel's hatred, the two soon begin their retreats, in which meeting in churches (even at Patara, their seaside haven, they explore the church) plays a large part. There can be no doubt that the inscription of the Christian incarnation on the roodscreen in St. Cuthbert's Philbeach Gardens, "Verbum caro factum est et habitavit in nobis" (The Word was made flesh and dwelt among us), is a powerful metaphor for the literal translation of the power of Eros (or of Aphrodite or of other ancient sacred powers) into their flesh and being.

When they finally reach Patara the sense of the sacred persists, and again art (Julian as Hamlet again) is called forth to reinforce it. After the frenzied rape which contains so much motivational content (Julian herself, Priscilla's recent but concealed death, Hamlet, an unshakeable sense of doom, the fury of Eros's image), the two are overwhelmed by a sense of being in a sacred space, surrounded by bad spirits. Julian, as BP had done earlier, goes through a metamorphosis and becomes for him a holy object:

> She looked so much, and beautifully, older, not the child I had known at all, but some wonderful holy woman, a prophetess, a temple prostitute. She had combed her hair down smoothly and pressed it back and her face had the nakedness, the solitude, the ambiguous staring eloquence of a mask. She had the dazed empty look of a great statue.

From their powerful experience for which religion serves so well as a metaphor, they both assume that they will write great books. The persistence of this idea and the belief that it is intense human love (Eros) that produces art are broken fairly quickly by BP's all too human lies and moral inadequacy, by his imperfection as an instrument.

In a very different context in *The Fire and the Sun*, Murdoch, in talking about Plato's long path to enlightenment, points to his fears that art is "a sham, a false transcendence, a false imitation of another world . . . where the veiled something which is sought and found is no more than a shadow out of the private storeroom of the personal unconscious." In this novel, where BP's moral progress somehow equals the progress towards good art, this is unfortunately the stage he has reached. Having achieved the intensity of love, he is imperfect in other dimensions, and so the far-reaching stories of Priscilla and of the Baffin-Christian enclave must take over. Because virtue and art are aligned in Murdoch's mind, the final developments take place as means to the knowledge of virtue, and the characters' progress is through guilt and punishment.

Priscilla's death, long in building and harrowingly well-prepared for, is inevitable as is Nina's in the early novel, *The Flight from the Enchanter*. In both cases, cries for help go unheard by a central character, so self-absorbed that, as BP puts it, "I had not got a grain of spirit to offer to any other person." When Priscilla is dead, BP in conversation with Francis realizes that the truth of the matter, "Priscilla died because nobody loved her," results from a fatal problem in BP's love for Julian. His perception of that love as divine and absolute, even when she is apparently lost to him, does not at all jibe with his failure to help Priscilla or to tell Julian about her death when he would rather put his false sexual "ordeal" first. Blindly he thinks his enlightenment has taken place, and that through Julian he has gone as far as he can:

> Her love for me was an absolute word spoken. It belongs to the eternal. I cannot doubt that word, it is the logos of all being, and if she loves me not chaos is come again. Love is knowledge, you see, like the philosophers always told us. I know her by intuition as if she were here inside my head. . . . Because I love Julian I ought to be able to love everybody. I will be able to one day.

To have been so wrong and to be in such agony over Priscilla's death and Julian's absence puzzles him, but it also sets him up for the real crisis: Rachel's murder of Arnold because of the letter the latter had written Christian. How Murdochian and clever this plot turn is, and yet how absolutely and ingeniously dependent upon causality!

BP's trial for Arnold's murder arouses the reader against the perfidy of Rachel, but it also provides the final irony of the novel. In his magnificent postscript, BP says that this unexpected, dreadful and objectively unjust public humiliation and the myriad guilt feelings it arouses in him are the real point of his life, whereas all his other ideas of transformation, new being, ordeal, etc. had been chimerical:

> I had been confronted (at last) with a sizeable *ordeal* labelled with my name. This was not something to be wasted. I had never felt more alert and alive in my life, and from the vantage point of my new consciousness I looked back upon what I had been: a timid incomplete resentful man.

and

> I also felt something like this, that the emergence of my life out of quietness into public drama and horror was a necessary and in some deep sense natural outcome of the visitation with which I had been honoured. Sometimes I thought of it as a punishment for the failure of my vow of silence. Sometimes, shifting the same idea only very slightly, it seemed more like a reward.

The trial comprehends the real flaying and leads BP to the "writing" of the present book, to his education by P. Loxias, to his real metamorphosis. Because of this trial the primary persona of BP is replaced by a new man whose existence modifies and improves the narrowly structured artwork that his autobiography would have been.

No longer lost in ignorance and darkness. BP now knows what the silence is which he had, in his blindness, identified as some calm of mind at the writing desk with the creative Eros hovering over him. In one of the most subtle paragraphs of the novel, Murdoch, through BP's final address to Loxias, gives us the full substance of the novel she has written:

> So we live on together here in our quiet monastery, as we are pleased to call it. And so I come to the end of this book. I do not know if I shall write another. You have taught me to live in the present and to forswear the fruitless anxious pain which binds to past and to future our miserable local arc of the great wheel of desire. Art is a vain and hollow show, a toy of gross illusion, unless it points beyond itself and moves ever whither it

points. You who are a musician have shown me this, in the wordless ultimate regions of your art, where form and substance hover upon the brink of silence, and where articulate forms negate themselves and vanish into ecstasy. Whether words can travel that path through truth, absurdity, simplicity, to silence I do not know, nor what the path can be like. I may write again. Or may at last abjure what you have made me see to be but a rough magic.

Art's pointing beyond itself, its hovering of form and substance (finally united in Apollo's music) upon the brink of silence, its negating and vanishing into ecstasy, are all part of Murdoch's stringent concept of the good which can be perceived only as unknown, wholly other, silent. The high claim for art that she makes is that at its best, when not blinded by illusion, this is the end to which it points. BP is Murdoch's metaphor for the stages of art, and he has here reached the final step in the human knowledge that can be conveyed by art functioning at its purest.

What remains for BP is the question of whether he will write again or, like Prospero, "abjure this rough magic." Because in this paradoxical book he has gradually, progressively and finally become, for all his realism as a character, the symbol for the farthest reaches of art, Murdoch chooses the path of abjuration, and he passes on to silence. After the betraying, amusing, point-of-view obscuring postscripts of the other characters, P. Loxias chastises them, and then settles in to a description of BP's death. "The false god punishes, the true god slays." Murdoch's concentration on death as the real subject to be studied (see Socrates, of course) is brought into serious, ironic play here. Art points beyond itself to the void, to death, and thence her symbol BP travels. The last few sentences of the book and of P. Loxias's postscript are fraught with understatement even as they comprehend the novel's whole thought pattern of progress from bad art to real art to the "nothing" which human beings, with their flawed sense of duration in seeing the reality that death reveals, so ardently turn aside from: "Art is not cosy and it is not mocked. Art tells the only truth that ultimately matters. It is the light by which human things can be mended. And after art there is, let me assure you all, nothing."

And yet, the paradoxes remain. The reader's uncertain sense of BP from the other characters' postscripts makes him somehow still a figure of fun and absurdity, and according to P. Loxias, art celebrates this and because of it can be seen as made up of adventure stories. The idea is tied up with Murdoch's sense of fiction as a reflection of mankind's activity in the world,

where novel plots at their best are spun from the tragicomic doings of
characters who live and love their adventures. The artist's job at its highest
includes the transmission of those adventures with as much energy and
excitement as possible to an audience eager to be absorbed by the pleasures
of the tale; hence BP dies wishing he had written not *Hamlet* but *Treasure
Island*. As Loxias says of art, "At an austere philosophy it can only mock."
Although it points to death, this novel does not break its comedic frame to
wallow in tragedy and, even more pointedly, it does not lose its feeling of
realism. In one of his last tricks, Loxias-Apollo claims that he has the real
amulets—the water buffalo lady bronze and the Victorian snuff box inscribed
"A Friend's Gift"—on his desk; they do indeed exist as did Bradley Pearson,
as does he. This final sleight of hand joins the fictional to the real in an
oddly convincing way; even though, as he points out, some may claim that
both BP and Loxias are "simply fictions, the inventions of a minor novelist"
(tongue-in-cheek Murdoch), their triumphant life in the high realm of reality
exists. BP himself, in his postscript, expresses the central paradox in Murdoch's work. Torn out of himself by the hands of the terrible transforming
godhead of reality, he remembers Plato's injunction against the artist, and
observes that Socrates and Christ wrote nothing:

> And yet: I am writing these words and others whom I do not
> know will read them. With and by this paradox I have lived,
> dear friend, in our sequestered peace. Perhaps it will always be
> for some an unavoidable paradox, but one which is only truly
> lived when it is also a martyrdom.

The martyrdom (another concept the early BP misunderstood) coexists with
life and creativity, silence with words.

And with what Dionysian energy Murdoch has spun her web of words.
Every technique in her considerable arsenal is displayed: false beginnings,
false and real endings, *peripeteia*, strong and often amusing image patterns,
mythological interweaving, precise, causally worked-out ideology, brilliant
conversations, ironic letters, profound ruminations and high comedy all
coalesce in this most difficult and fruitful of novels. In no other book has
she taken a character so far, from irritating inadequacy to the absolute of
art and thence to death, and never is she as positive and generous in that
journey as she is with Bradley Pearson. The result is an affirmation which
one must feel even on a first, superficial reading. Although the supercilious,
self-absorbed Julian may remark on reading the manuscript of the story, "A
literary failure," the detached reader of this whole and subtle novel surely
cannot agree.

RICHARD TODD

A Word Child

At first glance *A Word Child* seems to raise familiar themes in familiar ways, but a closer look reveals some differences and developments from its predecessors. It should be stressed that in this novel, too, there is a relationship to material which has been aired by Murdoch in a nonliterary, polemic context. In 1975, the year of publication of *A Word Child,* Murdoch contributed to one of a series of *Black Papers* arguing against government education policy in Britain, insofar as it seemed to favour the indiscriminate introduction of nonselective, unstreamed comprehensivization. At the end of this essay she urges that there is room for complacency in the face of such a state of affairs only as far as able, middle-class children "with moderately bookish homes and educationally ambitious parents behind them" are concerned; she is manifestly worried about the fate of "the poor clever children with an illiterate background who on the 'chance' system are being denied the *right* to a strict academic education which can only be achieved on the basis of some sort of selection." The narrator of *A Word Child* comes from this latter background; Murdoch characteristically shows how strong even under the "old" system the element of chance is, and at one level the narrative can be seen as examining or even challenging some of the theoretical assumptions of the *Black Paper* essay.

Hilary, a prostitute's child from an illiterate and almost utterly loveless background, has been "rescued" because of the discovery of his linguistic aptitude by the schoolmaster Mr. Osmand, a version—as practically always in Murdoch—of the good man. Hilary proceeded to pursue his study at

From *Iris Murdoch.* © 1984 by Richard Todd. Methuen & Co. Ltd., 1984. Originally entitled *"The Nice and the Good* to *A Word Child."*

Oxford with considerable success. While there he encountered and was befriended by Gunnar and Anne Jopling, who had also shown unwonted kindness to his half-sister Crystal, with whom Hilary describes himself as "oned in love." Mr. Osmand appears only once in the novel, apparently *in extremis*, but it is entirely characteristic of Hilary's peculiarly appalling form of willed accident-proneness that he is unfit to help Osmand on this occasion, having (unaccustomedly) "tripped out" through the hospitality of his flat-mate, the ex-pop-star Christopher. Osmand is later discovered to have committed suicide, as we learn through a letter from his landlady. It is worth pausing to note again the decorative level at which Murdoch is capable of orchestrating a theme, in this case literacy: among the letters interspersed throughout Hilary's narrative are ones from this landlady, from Crystal to her "dull swain" Arthur Fisch, and from Lady Kitty Jopling to Hilary. In their ascending order of literacy these posit, through the particular instance, the difficulty of arriving at general truths about the complexity of the relationship between social standing, intelligence and education. Even Lady Kitty is unable to spell "providence" and "psychoanalyst." In general, Murdoch's control over narrative voice and register, either in epistolary form or by means of devices such as the postscripts to *The Black Prince,* is not always sufficiently appreciated.

The relationship between Hilary and Gunnar is really central to the narrative, clear yet surrounded by mystery. It is reminiscent of, yet different from, familiar forms of the artist-saint contrast: here, as with *Henry and Cato* (1976), we seem to be watching not so much the artist in one protagonist and the saint in another as a composite of artist and saint in each protagonist, the contrast now lying more explicitly in the social and spiritual circumstances of each protagonist. A reader is prompted, as on previous occasions, to ponder the extent to which the relationship is sublimated and homosexual, with many of the other characters—in this instance Gunnar's two wives particularly—acting as unacknowledged substitutes. Certainly many of the relationships in *A Word Child* exist in an uneasily shifting equilibrium, different from the cool exchanges of, for instance, *A Severed Head;* one thinks particularly perhaps of the complex triangle involving Laura Impiatt, Christopher Cather and Clifford Larr. This is comically compounded by Laura's insistences, and Hilary's denials, that Hilary is in love with her: what is characteristic here is what may be thought of as a new uncertainty on the part of the author.

While at Oxford Hilary had precipitated, on his own account, a catastrophe which had ended his and Gunnar's careers there, though Gunnar had subsequently made more of an ostensible "success" of his life. Hilary, falling desperately in love with Anne, had at last tried to persuade her to leave

Gunnar and their young son Tristram. Anne, frightened and confused by her recent discovery that she is once more pregnant, had provoked Hilary into crashing the car on the "motorway" (a curious anachronism). Hilary had been seriously injured and Anne killed. Much later, Hilary discovers that Gunnar, contrary to what Anne had told him, apparently never knew, or at least had never said to anyone, that she was pregnant. Had she therefore been carrying Hilary's child? The novel provides no answer, though the possibility that she had underlines the humorous potential of the present situation:

> It suddenly struck me as comic . . . that I was now being bad-gered by three childless women in their thirties, two wanting me to present them with a child, the other wanting me to sanction her marriage. Child-hunger seemed to be the thing just now.

Hilary and Gunnar are both haunted and obsessed by their past, and the extent to which the attempted intermediation of Gunnar's second wife is purely selfless remains doubtful to the reader: Murdoch here skilfully distinguishes between Hilary's fantasy apprehension of and utter trust in Lady Kitty, and a reader's ability to see, as Hilary cannot, the preposter-ousness of much of her behaviour including her final suggestion that Hilary should provide her with a child. Tristram had earlier committed suicide and Gunnar, as an apparent side-effect of a later operation is, according to Lady Kitty, sterile. Thus Hilary, having already fallen in love with Lady Kitty, appears to be entering compulsively on a course of action identical to that which had earlier proved so destructive. Ironically and disastrously, Gunnar, who was supposed to have been away, enters the scene of the last meeting between Hilary and Kitty, in which Hilary had resolved to bring the matter to an end: in a riverside scuffle neither man is injured, but Lady Kitty, falling off a jetty, subsequently dies of exposure. Hilary later discovers that he has been unwittingly betrayed by his jealous fiancée Tommy.

The plot is not as mechanical as a summary description makes it sound, since Hilary's compulsive nature is illustrated through the narrative, which is not divided into chapters but arranged as a retrospective "diary," divided into days, which reflect the rigidness of the only way Hilary seems capable of dealing with his life. The surrounding characters assert their independence surprisingly feebly against Hilary's imposed regime, yet he is capable, too, of violently spontaneous action, such as ripping the telephone out of the wall. (Telephones are repeatedly invested with nightmare attributes in the Murdoch world.) The status quo of Hilary's life is seen as a series of contrived, repeated actions: crisis is foreshadowed by spontaneity.

Elizabeth Dipple has usefully discussed the relationship between *A Word*

Child and J.M. Barrie's *Peter Pan* (1904), a work consistently fascinating to Murdoch and to which there are many allusions in this novel. Dipple has noted that apart from various local decorations the mode of allusion has much to do with the predilection of many of the novel's characters for offering interpretations of *Peter Pan*, frequently as a spiritual allegory. She also draws attention to the functionality, in terms of Hilary's background, served by this and the other pieces of literature he carries around with him "almost as lucky charms." It may be thought, too, that in certain respects this novel brings the Shakespearian phase in Murdoch's development to an end, at least insofar as from now on there seems to be a less explicit concern with Shakespearian comic form, and a trend towards a more playful deployment of Shakespearian elements as other interests begin to take on a more dominant role. In *A Word Child*, *King Lear* and Murdoch's reading of that play are present in the comic wantonness of an ending in which Hilary, having resolved to "sing like birds in the cage" with Crystal, finds himself in the very next section witnessing her marriage to Arthur. Events in the novel come to support what Hilary has earlier been made to say about his involvement with the Joplings: "it was not a tragedy. I had not even the consolation of that way of picturing the matter. Tragedy belongs in art. Life has no tragedies."

Chronology

<table>
<tr><td>1919</td><td>Born in Dublin, July 15, daughter of Irene Alice Richardson and Wills John Hughes.</td></tr>
<tr><td>1938–42</td><td>Somerville College, Oxford. First-class honors, classical "Greats."</td></tr>
<tr><td>1942–44</td><td>Assistant Principal, British Treasury.</td></tr>
<tr><td>1944–46</td><td>Administrative Officer, UNRRA, working in London, Belgium, and Austria.</td></tr>
<tr><td>1947–48</td><td>Sarah Smithson Student in philosophy, Newnham College, Cambridge.</td></tr>
<tr><td>1948</td><td>Appointed Fellow of St. Anne's College, Oxford, and University Lecturer in Philosophy.</td></tr>
<tr><td>1953</td><td>Sartre: Romantic Rationalist.</td></tr>
<tr><td>1954</td><td>Under the Net.</td></tr>
<tr><td>1956</td><td>Marries John Oliver Bayley, Fellow of New College, Oxford. The Flight from the Enchanter.</td></tr>
<tr><td>1957</td><td>The Sandcastle.</td></tr>
<tr><td>1958</td><td>The Bell.</td></tr>
<tr><td>1959</td><td>Visits America to lecture at Yale University.</td></tr>
<tr><td>1961</td><td>A Severed Head. Dramatized with J. B. Priestley and performed 1963. Published 1964.</td></tr>
<tr><td>1962</td><td>An Unofficial Rose.</td></tr>
<tr><td>1963</td><td>The Unicorn.</td></tr>
</table>

1964   *The Italian Girl.*

1965   *The Red and the Green.*

1966   *The Time of the Angels.*

1968   *The Nice and the Good.*

1969   *Bruno's Dream.*

1970   *A Fairly Honourable Defeat, The Sovereignty of Good,* and *The Servants and the Snow* (play).

1971   *An Accidental Man.*

1972   *The Three Arrows.*

1973   *The Black Prince.*

1974   *The Sacred and Profane Love Machine.*

1975   *A Word Child.*

1976   *Henry and Cato.*

1977   *The Fire and the Sun: Why Plato Banished the Artists.*

1978   *The Sea, The Sea.*

1980   *Nuns and Soldiers.*

1983   *The Philosopher's Pupil.*

1986   *The Good Apprentice.*

Contributors

HAROLD BLOOM, Sterling Professor of the Humanities at Yale University, is the author of *The Anxiety of Influence*, *Poetry and Repression*, and many other volumes of literary criticism. His forthcoming study, *Freud: Transference and Authority*, attempts a full-scale reading of all of Freud's major writings. A MacArthur Prize Fellow, he is general editor of five series of literary criticism published by Chelsea House.

FREDERICK J. HOFFMAN is the author of *Freudianism and the Literary Mind*, *Gertrude Stein*, and *Imagination's New Beginning: Theology and Modern Literature*.

FRANK KERMODE is Professor of English at Columbia University. He is the author of *D. H. Lawrence*, *The Sense of an Ending*, and *The Genesis of Secrecy: On the Interpretation of Narrative*.

FRANK BALDANZA is Associate Professor of English at Bowling Green University. He is the author of a study of Ivy Compton-Burnett.

LOUIS L. MARTZ is Sterling Professor of English Emeritus at Yale University. His books include *John Donne in Meditation* and *Poet of Exile: A Study of Milton's Poetry*.

DONNA GERSTENBERGER is Professor of English at the University of Washington. She has co-edited a volume of American and British poetry.

ZOHREH TAWAKULI SULLIVAN is Assistant Professor of English at the University of Illinois, Champaign-Urbana.

A. S. BYATT is a writer and critic. Her books include *Wordsworth and Coleridge in Their Time* and *Iris Murdoch*.

STEVEN G. KELLMAN is Associate Professor of Comparative Literature at the University of Texas, San Antonio. He is the author of *The Self-Begetting Novel*.

ANN GOSSMAN teaches English at Texas Christian University.

LORNA SAGE is a journalist and critic. She is the author of *Doris Lessing*.

DOROTHY A. WINSOR teaches in the department of English at the Detroit College of Business.

ELIZABETH DIPPLE is Professor of English at Northwestern University. She is the author of *Iris Murdoch: Work for the Spirit*.

RICHARD TODD teaches English at the University of Amsterdam. His books include *Iris Murdoch: The Shakespearean Interest* and *Iris Murdoch*.

Bibliography

Baldanza, Frank. *Iris Murdoch*. New York: Twayne Publishers, Inc., 1974.

Berthoff, Warner. "Fortunes of the Novel: Muriel Spark and Iris Murdoch." *Massachusetts Review* 8 (1967): 301–32.

Bradbury, Malcolm. *Possibilities: Essays on the State of the Novel*. London: Oxford University Press, 1973.

Byatt, A. S. *Degrees of Freedom: The Novels of Iris Murdoch*. London: Chatto and Windus, 1965.

Cohan, Stevan. "From Subtext to Dream Text: The Brutal Egoism of Iris Murdoch's Male Narrators." *Women and Literature* 2 (1982): 222–42.

Fletcher, John. "Cheating the Dark Gods: Iris Murdoch and Racine." *International Fiction Review* 6 (Winter 1969): 75–76.

German, Howard. "The Range of Allusions in the Novels of Iris Murdoch." *Journal of Modern Literature* 2, no. 1 (September 1971): 57–85.

Hague, Angela. *Iris Murdoch's Comic Vision*. London: Associated University Presses, 1984.

Hoffman, Frederick J. "Iris Murdoch: The Reality of Persons." *Critique* 7, no. 1 (Spring 1964): 48–57.

Martin, Graham. "Iris Murdoch and the Symbolist Novel." *The British Journal of Aesthetics* 5, no. 3 (July 1965): 296–99.

Modern Fiction Studies 15 (1969). Iris Murdoch Special Issue.

Morrell, Roy. "Iris Murdoch—The Early Novels." *Critical Quarterly* 9, no. 3 (Autumn 1967): 272–82.

Obumselu, Ben. "Iris Murdoch and Sartre." *ELH* 42, no. 2 (Summer 1975): 296–317.

Pearson, Gabriel. "Iris Murdoch and the Romantic Novel." *New Left Review* 13–14 (January–April 1962): 137–45.

Rabinovitz, Rubin. *Iris Murdoch*. New York: Columbia University Press, 1968.

Ricks, Christopher. "A Sort of Mystery Novel." *New Statesman* 22 (October 1965): 604–5.

Souvage, Jacques. "Symbol as Narrative Device: An Interpretation of Iris Murdoch's *The Bell*." *English Studies* 43, no. 2 (April 1962): 81–96.

———. "The Unresolved Tension: An Interpretation of Iris Murdoch's *Under the Net*." *Revue des langues vivantes* 26, no. 6 (1966): 420–30.

Todd, Richard. *Iris Murdoch: The Shakespearean Interest*. London: Vision, 1979.

———. "The Plausibility of *The Black Prince*." *Dutch Quarterly Review* 8, no. 2 (1978): 82–93.

Wolfe, Peter. *The Disciplined Heart: Iris Murdoch and Her Novels*. Columbia, Mo.: University of Missouri Press, 1966.

Acknowledgments

Introduction by Harold Bloom, first published in a slightly different version in *The New York Times Book Review* (January 12, 1986), © 1986 by Harold Bloom. Reprinted by permission.

"Against Dryness" (originally entitled "Against Dryness: A Polemical Sketch") by Iris Murdoch from *Encounter* 16, no. 1 (January 1961), © 1960/61 by *Encounter*, Ltd. Reprinted by permission.

"*The Italian Girl*" (originally entitled "The Miracle of Contingency: The Novels of Iris Murdoch") by Frederick J. Hoffman from *Shenandoah: The Washington and Lee Review* 17, no. 1 (Autumn 1965), © 1965 by Washington and Lee University. Reprinted by permission of the Editor.

"*Bruno's Dream*" (originally entitled "Iris Murdoch") by Frank Kermode from *Modern Essays* by Frank Kermode, © 1970 by Frank Kermode. Reprinted by permission of the author.

"*The Nice and the Good*" by Frank Baldanza from *Modern Fiction Studies* 15, no. 3 (Autumn 1969), © 1969 by Purdue Research Foundation, West Lafayette, Ind. Reprinted by permission.

"The London Novels" (originally entitled "Iris Murdoch: The London Novels") by Louis L. Martz from *Twentieth-Century Literature in Retrospect*, edited by Reuben A. Brower, © 1971 by the President and Fellows of Harvard College. Reprinted by permission of Harvard University Press.

"*The Red and the Green*" by Donna Gerstenberger from *Iris Murdoch* by Donna Gerstenberger, © 1975 by Associated University Presses, Inc. Reprinted by permission of the publisher.

"The Demonic: *The Flight from the Enchanter*" (originally entitled "Enchantment and the Demonic in Iris Murdoch: *The Flight from the Enchanter*") by Zohreh Tawakuli Sullivan from *The Midwest Quarterly* 16, no. 3 (April 1975), © 1975 by *The Midwest Quarterly*. Reprinted by permission.

"Shakespearean Plot in the Novels of Iris Murdoch" by A. S. Byatt from *Iris Murdoch* by A. S. Byatt, © 1976 by A. S. Byatt. Reprinted by permission.

"*Under the Net*: The Self-Begetting Novel" (originally entitled "Raising the Net: Iris Murdoch and the Tradition of the Self-Begetting Novel") by Steven G. Kellman from *English Studies* 57, no. 1 (February 1976), © 1976 by Swets & Zeitlinger B.V., Amsterdam. Reprinted by permission.

"Icons and Idols in *A Severed Head*" (originally entitled "Icons and Idols in Murdoch's *A Severed Head*") by Ann Gossman from *Critique: Studies in Modern Fiction* 18, no. 3 (1977), © 1977 by James Dean Young. Reprinted by permission.

"The Pursuit of Imperfection: *Henry and Cato*" (originally entitled "The Pursuit of Imperfection") by Lorna Sage from *Critical Quarterly* 19, no. 2 (Summer 1977), © 1977 by Manchester University Press. Reprinted by permission of Manchester University Press.

"Solipsistic Sexuality in Murdoch's Gothic Novels" (originally entitled "Solipsistic Sexuality in Iris Murdoch's Gothic Novels") by Dorothy A. Winsor from *Renascence* 34, no. 1 (Autumn 1981), © 1981 by *Renascence*. Reprinted by permission.

"*The Black Prince* and the Figure of Marsyas" (originally entitled "Art and Theory") by Elizabeth Dipple from *Iris Murdoch: Work for the Spirit* by Elizabeth Dipple, © 1982 by Elizabeth Dipple. Reprinted by permission.

"*A Word Child*" (originally entitled "*The Nice and the Good* to *A Word Child*") by Richard Todd from *Iris Murdoch* by Richard Todd, © 1984 by Richard Todd. Reprinted by permission of Methuen & Co. Ltd.

Index